The Little Book of

Tarot

A simplified approach

Second Edition

Mary Loughland

Copyright © 2018

All rights reserved. This book or any portion thereof may not be reproduced or used in any manner whatsoever without the express written permission of the author except for the use of brief quotations in a book review.

Printed in Australia
First Printing, 2019
Second Edition
ISBN: 978-0-6486892-9-4
Illustrations from the Radiant Rider-Waite Tarot Deck® reproduced by permission of U.S. Games Systems, Inc., Stamford, CT 06902 USA. Copyright ©2006 by U.S. Games Systems, Inc. Further reproduction prohibited.

White Light Publishing
Melton, VIC, Australia 3337
www.whitelightpublishing.com.au

This book is dedicated to my family in spirit. I could not have done it without you.

Mary's Story

My awareness of spirit began when I was about seven years old. I would lay awake at night and could see the silhouette of a small boy near my bed. All he would do is kick a soccer ball at me, just wanting to play. Feeling frightened by the daily visits of this child, I told my mum who promptly went to see her psychic medium. The psychic (without any information from my mother) said that I had a little boy spirit in my room of similar age and that he would have passed as a baby or a stillborn close to my age. She then asked my mother for confirmation. Sadly, we did have a stillborn baby in the family who had passed close to when I was born. The child wanted to be acknowledged and just wanted to play with someone of similar age.

The fact that I could see my cousin who looked like he was of similar age to me despite passing at birth, showed that children do grow in spirit. That is my truth as I know it. It may be different for others. I have a love of the saying "whatever you believe will be true for you".

By the time I was ten, I had purchased my own pack of tarot cards, books on astrology and divination, and anything to do with the paranormal. I would avidly watch Karen Moregold and Athena Starwoman to learn how they interpreted planetary movements. I would also do the voiceovers pretending I was on TV and aspired to be the one reading the stars on telly one day.

At twelve, I took astrology classes over a two-year period to gain more insight. Looking back now, that's pretty weird for a thirteen-year-old, but I owe such gratitude to my father who drove me there every Friday night and my mother for being left alone at the end of each week while he waited in the car for the classes to finish.

My mum's psychic also predicted that I would be doing similar work to her, and she gave me some lessons with Italian playing cards to further ignite my psychic abilities.

I started to read professionally at twenty-one after receiving a reading from Trish who owned Reading Shops in Brisbane. She looked up from the reading she was doing for me and said, "You are going to work for me". I began reading in Toowong Village and Brisbane Myer Centre one month later. I owe my reading career to this incredible lady and mentor, who took a twenty-year-old under her wing and believed in me.

Fast forward to 2017 and I am working as a full time Psychic Medium, Reiki Master/Teacher and Tarot teacher. I post daily cards on Facebook to an audience of over 135,000 followers each day and my inbox is always overflowing with messages of gratitude from people who are looking for guidance and inspiration. I appear regularly on Psychic TV Australia, as predicted by my mum's psychic. My journey has reflected my childhood dream of working as a visionary and illuminating the path for others to bring healing and guidance. I combine my working knowledge of both astrology and tarot to provide insightful and comprehensive readings. I love teaching tarot as a tool to ignite and strengthen the psychic muscle.

After forty years of reading and continual learning, it still blows me away how it all comes together to tell a story, and often predicts events without us really knowing exactly how it works. The tarot is a tool to zone into another consciousness. In this state, you connect to other realms, connect to passed over spirit or guides that want to assist with your spiritual growth, and to shine light onto your path.

It has been an incredible journey of trust.

Introduction

The Little Book of Tarot arose from a need within me to share my knowledge of tarot in a very simplistic way. I wanted to write a book to teach tarot in a way that allows the tarot cards to talk to you. You will find this book to be to the point and written in language that you can use and apply to everyday life. When I was learning, I wanted a book that I could relate to. I wanted to know which cards meant I was making a crappy choice or whether I was following the best path. I wanted to know how cards worked in relation to one another. I wanted to be able to read a book cover to cover and not drown in information overload.

Tarot is a journey and you never stop learning. This book is for both the beginner and the advanced reader, as there is always something new to learn or refresh your knowledge in. Every time you pick up a tarot book you will glean a new meaning or see a card in a new perspective. You may have issues with certain cards from time to time and that is okay - there is no right or wrong. Just move on from it. If it doesn't talk to you, it doesn't talk to you. There will always be another time.

We will briefly cover the history of tarot, but let's delve straight into the card meanings, card combinations, blending cards to heighten or diminish meanings, spiritual practices and protection, astrology and numerology associations, spreads, time predictions and case studies to explain spreads and card combinations.

My aim in the Little Book of Tarot is to get your deck talking to you. Whilst there are basic meanings to all the cards, ultimately you will attune your energy to your chosen deck and the meanings you give to the cards will fall into patterns only you will understand and be able to read. That is the beauty of tarot.

If you find yourself unable to read cards in conjunction with other cards, or to tell a story by the end of the book, you will be able blend the card meanings, so they become "buzzwords" or create card combos that describe events and give more detail or accuracy. Blending and connecting cards and being guided by your intuition will result in fabulous readings. Tarot is a tool to develop intuition and psychic abilities and is often the link to other realms of consciousness that we really do not understand and perhaps, never will. Many tarot students will have a thirst for spiritual knowledge and will go onto develop mediumship and healing skills.

The Little Book of Tarot will help you connect the dots to tell a story. It will help you overcome the blocks you may have of getting it 'right' or 'wrong'. It will support you in your journey to see tarot as a tool to talk to you, to guide you on your path, or to give guidance to others - whether that be friends, family or even clients you read for professionally. You will learn to master techniques and spreads so that you can ace readings each and every time. You will gain confidence and trust in the messages you are receiving, that will see others seeking your advice and guidance over and over again. Let's get straight into it. I promise I won't get too technical or bore you with too much history. Just have a bit of patience, and we'll get to the juicy parts soon.

Mary

Contents

History   13
The Basics   15
Getting Started   17

Major Arcana
The Fool   27
The Magician   31
The High Priestess   35
The Empress   39
The Emperor   43
The Hierophant   45
The Lovers   49
The Chariot   53
Strength   55
The Hermit   59
The Wheel of Fortune   61
Justice   63
The Hanged Man   67
Death   71
Temperance   75
The Devil   77
The Tower   79
The Star   83
The Moon   85
The Sun   89
Judgement   91
The World   93

Court Cards
Page of Cups   99
Knight of Cups   101
Queen of Cups   103
King of Cups   107

Page of Pentacles	111
Knight of Pentacles	113
Queen of Pentacles	115
King of Pentacles	119
Page of Swords	121
Knight of Swords	123
Queen of Swords	125
King of Swords	129
Page of Wands	133
Knight of Wands	135
Queen of Wands	137
King of Wands	139

Minor Arcana

<u>Wands</u>

Ace of Wands	147
Two of Wands	149
Three of Wands	151
Four of Wands	153
Five of Wands	155
Six of Wands	157
Seven of Wands	159
Eight of Wands	161
Nine of Wands	163
Ten of Wands	165

<u>Cups</u>

Ace of Cups	167
Two of Cups	169
Three of Cups	171
Four of Cups	173
Five of Cups	175
Six of Cups	177
Seven of Cups	179
Eight of Cups	181
Nine of Cups	183

Ten of Cups   185

Swords
Ace of Swords   187
Two of Swords   189
Three of Swords   191
Four of Swords   193
Five of Swords   195
Six of Swords   197
Seven of Swords   199
Eight of Swords   203
Nine of Swords   205
Ten of Swords   207

Pentacles
Ace of Pentacles   209
Two of Pentacles   211
Three of Pentacles   213
Four of Pentacles   215
Five of Pentacles   217
Six of Pentacles   219
Seven of Pentacles Eight   221
of Pentacles   223
Nine of Pentacles   225
Ten of Pentacles   227

Blending or Linking   229
Cards Rephrasing   233
Questions

Card Spreads
Celtic Spread   239
Question Spread   243
Yes or No Questions   247
Horseshoe Spread   249
Astrology Spread   253
Relationship Spread   259

Helpful Tips 265
Keywords 269

History

There is a lot of colourful speculation concerning the origins of tarot. What seem to be the earliest existing tarot cards date back to circa 1400. One of the earliest decks is the Visconti deck which was commissioned by the Duke of Milan from an Italian artist called Bonifacio Bembo. The deck was named after the Duke's family name.

The original purpose of tarot cards was to play games. The game of tarot has many cultural variations. Tarocchini is what the tarot game is called in Italy and was played mostly in Bologna but was played as far south as Sicily. The eighteenth century saw tarot's greatest revival where it became the most popular card game in France and Central Europe; played everywhere except British Isles.

Tarot was also used for divinatory and occult purposes and there is some evidence to suggest that by the mid-eighteenth century, the divinatory and occult influences for cards had spread from Italy to other parts of Europe. In France, writer Antoine Court de Gébelin declared that the tarot was based on a sacred book written by Egyptian priests and brought to Europe by gypsies. There is a lot of inaccuracy and unknown facts about the actual origins, however this does not detract from the power of the tarot. We do not really need to know the history to benefit or use the tarot to delve into the unconscious or use it for divinatory means.

Fast forward to 1909 and the most common deck is printed - the famous Rider-Waite deck. The Rider Waite name is derived from publisher William Rider and scholarly mystic A.E. Waite. Pamela Colman Smith was commissioned to illustrate the deck based on the instruction of AE Waite. The deck is sometimes referred to Rider Waite Smith, but lovingly referred to as the "Rider" universally. The Rider-Waite deck was designed for divination and included a book written by Waite in which he explained much of the esoteric meaning behind the imagery. This revolutionized tarot and is considered the first modern deck. Colman's detailed imagery in the Minor Arcana allows the student to connect intuitively to the messages to tell a story.

The Basics

The tarot deck is made up of seventy-eight cards, which include twenty-two major arcana cards and fifty-six minor arcana cards.

The major arcana cards consist of twenty-two cards which deal with spiritual life lessons and archetypes. Major arcana cards describe major life changes and turning points in our life for example, births, marriage, jobs, challenges etc. They also represent the symbolism from birth to old age. In a reading, always look for the major cards first as they will tell you where the big changes are happening or where the lessons are.

The biggest part of the deck is the minor arcana. While the major arcana deals with the major milestones of the journey of life, the minor arcana represents four smaller cycles, each numbered Ace through Ten, and followed by four court cards (Page, Knight, Queen, King). While many readers feel that majors indicate strong areas of concern or strength in a reading, the minors are still important to show the full picture.

There are four suits in the minor arcana, and each suit represents one of the four elements (Fire, Air, Earth, and Water). The minor cards will give you the detail in a reading and describe the people that help or hinder your life through the appearance of the court cards, so they are just as important as the major cards. So, out of all that, the majors are the big milestones or changes and the minors will give you the detail. If you have no majors in a spread, it will be day to day activities and things you have control over. If you have more major cards, the hands of fate may play a bigger role or have a significant impact on the person you are reading for. We traditionally call the person you are reading for the 'querent' but are more commonly known as your client or the person being read.

Getting Started

What do you need to get started?
- A Rider Waite Tarot deck (preferably) or a similar deck, so the information or images resonate without having to translate the information in your head.
- Silk scarf or special box to keep your cards.
- A couple of good tarot reference books while you are learning the meanings. This is a personal choice and you are not going to find everything in one book, so get that out of your head right now. Different teachers have different perspectives and you will blend all that knowledge and mould it into your own style.

The easiest method to learning the meanings is to write down the seventy-eight cards and remember one or two key words. You can also do this for reversed or inversed cards if you choose. I have included 'key word' pages in this book for you to scribble down meanings. Use a pencil, as you may revise meanings from time to time depending on your mood or the feedback you receive. Don't worry if you can't remember the meanings; look at the images and write down what you feel. Remember there is no right or wrong. It is an intuitive practice. You need to learn the meanings, but don't get hung up about it. I do not use reversed cards but will read them reversed if it pops out that way. I have given reversed card meanings in the summary sheets if you wish to use them. If a card doesn't talk to you, move on to the next card. You may want to meditate on it or put it under your pillow for a few days. You will eventually give it a meaning.

Before any reading, you need to quiet your mind; either through meditation or practicing grounding techniques. You can do guided visualizations like meeting your guide, or just focus on stilling your mind so you can be a clear channel for messages you are about to receive using the tarot. Most of us though, do not have time for meditation prior to a reading, so you'll want to perform a sacred practice to ground your energy, so you can be a clear channel. You will know if you are not grounded, as you may look at cards and draw a blank, or they simply won't make sense at all. Try meditating to see if there is a difference or leave it that day as there might be too much going on in your world.

Choose an area in your home that is away from noise and distractions. You can set up your own little ritual, such as burning incense, sage, oil etc. and create your own sacred space for doing your readings. A ritual is beneficial because it sets you up for the frame of mind to read, and to create the sacred space for information and guidance to channel through.

Take your cards out of the silk or box. I like to lay my cards on my silk scarf. Some of you may prefer to do it on a wooden table. There is no right or wrong; whatever feels right for you. I also use a largish rose quartz crystal and I tap my cards three times. Rose quartz is the stone for love, and I like to infuse my cards with love for the highest good of my client or myself, or whoever I am reading for. I say a prayer of intention that my reading is for the highest good and thank my guides and passed over loved ones who help me during my readings to relay information that is helpful, insightful and gives clarity. Always remember that when we are reading, we are often looking for clarity, insight or reassurance about our life direction and path. I also thank my guides for their divine protection always.

If I am reading for myself, I shuffle my cards, then I personally cut them in eight piles. You may just want to cut it twice. This is to ensure any previous energy has been removed. I also look at the bottom card from the pile as that will generally tell me the focus for the reading. Then, I shuffle them again until I get the feeling I'm ready. I cut the cards in two piles and I always choose the pile on the *right*. If I have a client with me, I shuffle the cards first, I cut them to make sure any previous energy has been cleared, and then hand them to the client to shuffle. Please note: not all readers like other people touching their cards; it's a personal choice. When the client is ready, ask them to hand you back the cards. Then, ask them to cut the deck and choose the pile to read from. If you are reading for yourself, just follow the same practice. If you are doing an email reading, you can ask the client for a photo and date of birth. Their date of birth is just so you can choose a significator (based on the person's star sign - usually a court card that describes the person). I'll talk more about what a significator is later in the book.

Note: You can buy your own cards. They do not have to be gifted. I have always bought my own.

Although we have not been through all the meanings, I feel it's important before you start reading, to work out what you are prepared to read about, and what is against your own personal code of ethics.

On my website www.marytarotreadings.com you will find my code of ethics. For legal purposes, you must state that readings are for guidance only and that one should consult the appropriate health, financial, or legal professionals in all instances. I also keep Lifeline and other helpline numbers on hand, as sometimes people need the help of qualified professionals like counsellors etc. Be mindful of how you deliver messages, as you don't know the state of mind of the person you are reading for. Your role as a reader is to be kind, compassionate and empathetic. This is not to say that you should fabricate the reading in anyway, as sometimes you get what you get, but your aim is to make the person feel better for having had the reading with you. If you see despair, point out the solution. You may supplement an oracle card for the spiritual solution. Tarot, in my opinion, tells us what the situation is, and the oracle cards can provide the spiritual solution. The tarot can give us the solution as well; usually in modern day language. It's simply a personal choice.

Sometimes you may draw a blank. That's okay - it happens to the best of us. Just be honest and say, "I'm sorry, I'm not picking up anything". You might ask how this is, if we are just reading cards. Well, that's the difference between a tarot reader and an intuitive or psychic reader who uses the cards as a prop. There is no right or wrong, but if you get a blank you are an intuitive reader and it's just not happening today. That's okay. I believe everyone has intuition and even if you think you are just reading card meanings, it will still resonate and be accurate, regardless. If you feel you should *not* read for someone, *don't*, as it will be more trouble than its worth. Trust your gut instincts always.

My aim in this little book is to teach you the basic meanings and help you build a relationship with your cards. I want you to become inspired readers, not 'cut and paste meaning' readers. I want to see you flourish as readers, even if you don't want to do it professionally. I want you to 'get it' and you will. By the end of the book, you will get the feel of the reading and will see patterns, challenge areas and how card combos work, and how they heighten or diminish the meaning of the card.

One last thing - when you finish a reading, you can pass your cards through incense, sage etc. I also tap them three times with my rose quartz. I imagine myself cutting the energy chord from the last person / reading, so I invite fresh energy. You need to also re-ground between readings. Go outside, drink water, feel the earth under your feet. Say a prayer of thanks for the guidance you have received.

A word of advice: if you keep asking the same question over and over, the tarot can start to spit out garbage to say 'enough'. You will know it's not playing the game when it refuses to make sense. Just stop and give it a rest. You need to trust. Tarot is for guidance; not to be consulted every second of the day. You will be sent to Tarot Anonymous, of which I am the President.

This leads us to the meanings. Don't get overwhelmed in the meanings. I have 'goldfish syndrome', so I have kept the meanings concise and in everyday language that you can relate to. If you are anything like me, I like to learn quickly so I can use the knowledge to get cracking with my new tool or project straight away. If it takes me too long, I lose interest.

How the Tarot works

Tarot is a divinatory tool that mirrors your current situation and taps into universal energy to predict the likely outcome, based on the energies at play. In tarot, there is both free will and fate through the interpretation of the minor and major arcana. You can start off learning tarot by drawing a daily card each morning and reflecting each night on how that day played out and deciding what relevance that meaning had in reference to your day. You can journal or use the blank summary sheets at the back of the book to write down your keywords.

It is perfectly okay to read for yourself and when you gain confidence, to read for family and friends. I have had many students who have gone on to read professionally or use tarot in conjunction with other modalities.

MAJOR ARCANA

Major Arcana Overview

The Major Arcana represent life lessons that we experience in our journey of life. There are twenty-two cards numbered from 0 (The Fool) and ending at 21 (The World). They represent major milestones in life, such as life, death, marriage etc. Each of the major arcana cards that appear in a reading will draw your attention to the area of life that is or will be a focus. Each card has astrological and numerical associations that amplify the energy of the card.

We always scan our eye over a spread to see how many major cards there are. This will tell you which big things or themes are playing out. Look at what is next to those major cards - are they positive or negative? This will give you more detail or insight about the situation. The number of majors will tell you if anything significant is happening in a person's life - for example, the Death card will show a door closing and a new beginning. A person may be pushed out of a job and this may not be an easy path for the person in question. Or, the Tower may appear to shake up their foundations or show a house move. You may see the Hierophant appear for someone who is hoping to get married, as this is traditionally the commitment card that has religious overtones.

The major arcana cards are also known as archetypes. The major arcana is often depicted through the Fool's Journey, which is a metaphor for the journey of life. Each major arcana card stands for a stage on that journey; of the lessons we need to learn, our growth from those lessons, and challenges along the way. It encompasses both life and death, and the journey in-between.

You can get as deep as you want with tarot or use it as a tool for divination or self-growth. It's entirely up to you what you use it for.

THE FOOL

THE FOOL

Buzz Words: new beginning, new path, new journey, following your heart, childlike innocence and beliefs, what you do not have in experience you will make up for in enthusiasm and willingness to learn, spontaneity

General Meaning

The number of this card is 0 which stands for the continuous cycle of life, birth and death. Symbolically, the Fool is newly born and about to begin his search for the holy grail of spiritual enlightenment. He sets out on this perilous journey filled with hope and believing that anything is possible.

When the Fool appears in a reading, it relates to a new beginning. It is telling you to have faith with the innocence of a child and take a leap of faith. In a career reading, it suggests an industry totally new to you, or a role where you need to learn new skills. Remember, the Fool is at the beginning of the journey, so it relates to new experiences. Look towards surrounding cards to see if the new opportunity will bring challenges with it. For example, if you had the Fool followed by the Ten of Wands (burden), you would say there is a new beginning around the area of work, but it does come with a lot of extra work that could become a burden to you, so to take that into consideration.

If you are reading this as Reversed, it would mean you are taking a risk or throwing caution to the wind.

Finances

New ways of doing things or managing your funds differently. Investing in new ventures or property (this would be strengthened if you had the Ten of Pentacles or perhaps the Four of Wands, or any cards you may relate to real-estate or investments). Looking outside the square of what is normal for you. Expect to have a big learning curve as the Fool is at the beginning of his journey. With financial matters, I would suggest looking closely at what is next to the Fool - Has it got positive cards next to it? Are you taking a leap of faith, or are you being foolish? If the Devil was beside it, you may be being foolish. If the Sun was beside it, follow your heart, as it will lead to prosperity. You may need to look at things from a fresh perspective or do something different to get a different result.

Career

New opportunities or paths that could be in a different field to what your training is in. The Fool is about new beginnings that requires one to learn new skills or new ways of doing things. This contrasts with the new beginnings of the Magician, where new opportunities presented to you would be using the skills that you have because someone is after a person highly skilled in that particular area.

Love

Look towards surrounding cards, but take the buzzword and apply it, because you may need to be more spontaneous. It could be new love, but if you or the person you are reading for is in an existing relationship, you need to read it in that context. You may read it as exploring new ways to reconnect, or if single, it could indeed be new horizons or meeting new people. This card also does come up for sexuality of being bi sexual or gay if it is close to the High Priestess. This is not about judgement, it's about the tarot connecting to the person you are reading for and exploration of what comes up in a reading. When you are starting out, perhaps use the buzzwords of 'new horizons' first.

Health

Due to the connection with the Planet Uranus, there is a lot of nervous tension here. Denotes nervous tension/energy, great but undisciplined mental energy and unstable conditions of all types.

Card Combinations with the Fool

Devil: Reckless Addictive behaviour

Court Cards: Could mean that person is eccentric

Ace of Wands: New job in a new field

High Priestess: Hidden sexuality or wanting to express sexuality

Three of Swords: Don't be reckless with your words; it will cause tears

Sun: Take a leap of faith and it will work out perfectly. The Sun is shining down on this decision as there is synchronicity

You catch my drift with the card combos or blending. The combos are where accuracy lies.

As an Outcome Card

As an outcome card, the Fool would denote that the person you are reading for is going to start a new way of life or a new way of being. It may be a new job or could even be retirement. It is a new phase in one's life. As a major arcana card and an outcome card, it is positive as it brings fresh new energy and vitality to one's life and allows them to start again with a clean slate.

Astrological Association: Uranus

THE MAGICIAN

THE MAGICIAN

Buzz Words: specialist in field, leadership, new beginnings, new projects, manifesting, positive change, skills and resources, communication, advertising, marketing, writing, linguistic

General Meaning

When the Magician appears in a reading it talks about a new project; having the ability and skills to start something new. The Magician can be a person in your life that comes to lead or show you how something is done, hence he shows mastery in his chosen field. The Magician can signify that you may be required to step into leadership in a niche market or lead the way.

Around work, it relates to new projects, having the skills to do something new and hence a sense of power (remember knowledge and skill gives one power). He represents the ability to manifest what you desire. He is the Magician; he can and will make things happen.

In love, it tells you that that you have learnt from past mistakes and have the skills to work things out, but a need to apply what you know.

Finances

In financial matters, someone could be giving you specialized advice. You could be wanting to start fresh with saving or looking at investing in a new project. Money will be put aside for something new that you are planning.

Career

When the Magician appears in a career reading, expect positive change or new projects to come up. If a question is about a job, the Magician heralds a new beginning. Take the energy of the card - which is positive - take the buzzword - which is power and knowledge - and know that you or the person you are reading for in the career sector will more than likely have something new coming up. If you are feeling doubtful, know that you have the skills and resources you need to step up and do what needs to be done to get ahead. The Magician is the manifestation card, so know that it is within your power to create the changes you want to see. The power resides in you. At times, the Magician can appear as an entrepreneurial sort of person that may help you on your path.

Love

Now, in itself, it's not a romantic card, but you can use it as a word to connect to the energy around love life. It may be that you're starting something new. What do you need to do (because you know what to do, right?) to instill more passion in your life? If a court card appears next to the Magician, it does make it a bit easier, as long as it is not the Devil. If so, you need to run; just keep running or press the block and delete button quickly and move onto the next profile. But, the Magician could also turn up as a positive and influential person in your life. It could be describing a new start in your love and romantic life, whether one is married or single.

Health

Due to its association with Mercury, the Magician governs the central nervous system, lungs and five senses. The Magician coming up in a health reading could signify needing to see a 'specialist'.

Card Combinations with the Magician

King of Swords: Medical specialist
King of Swords/Three of Swords: Heart specialist
King of Swords/Empress: Gynecologist

King of Swords/Hermit: Psychiatrist (If it was just King of Swords with the Hermit, it would be a psychologist, however the Magician escalates the status to 'psychiatrist')

Chariot: Mechanic

Wheel of Fortune: Manifesting positive changes

Devil: Someone manipulative and using power for the detriment of others, depression, not thinking clearly, narcissistic tendencies

Moon: Reiki or Healer

High Priestess: Spiritual mentor or guide

World/Page of Swords: Journalist or someone who writes in the public eye. The Magician next to a card will exalt the meaning if positive, and if it relates to a court card or a Major Arcana card that represents a person, it will describe the characteristics of a person. The Magician is powerful.

As Outcome Card

It is a Major card, and it is a positive card giving positive outcomes and confidence in the direction that the client is wanting. If you are looking for a yes or no type of outcome, then the Magician is a Yes card in a positive sense or will bring about a positive outcome for the question asked.

Astrological Association: Mercury, which controls both Virgo and Gemini

THE HIGH PRIESTESS

Buzz Words: intuition, psychic, guidance, waiting, patience, answers yet to be revealed, mystic, secrets, hiding, wisdom, gut instincts

THE HIGH PRIESTESS

General Meaning

When the High Priestess appears, she asks you to be guided by your intuition and not your rational mind. She is the card of mystery, spiritual and psychic realms. Hidden wisdom and knowledge is coming to you, but you may need patience. This card comes up for study as well, hence the wisdom part. Sometimes in a man's reading, it can signify a woman he is about to get to know. but he is yet to get fully acquainted with. If the High Priestess falls alongside a court card, it will describe a person who is intuitive e.g. High Priestess and Queen of Cups would be an Empath.

Finances

You may need more information before you make a decision. You may need to trust your gut instincts if something does not feel right. Often, when relating to finances, the High Priestess will indicate that you do not have all the information, so do not make a decision until you do. You may also need to wait. Someone could be secretive regarding finances. The word secret or hidden is amplified with this card. What this would mean for a finance question is you need more information and do not go through with something until you are satisfied with the answers.

Career

Psychic or spiritual work may be of interest if this appears in the career section, or there could be secrets at your work place. If the Tower was following this, it would mean that there would be restructures or changes that no one knows about yet. But, in itself, the High Priestess in the career section would ask you to wait before making any decisions as again, you do not have all the information at hand and all you can go on is your gut instincts. People could indeed be keeping information from you, or you may be feeling that there is more to the story than what you know.

Love

Are you keeping secrets, or are secrets being kept from you? If you have positive cards close by, don't be alarmed, however the High Priestess is about trusting your gut instincts - about people and agendas - so if you are in a relationship, this could mean that you are not sharing your inner thoughts or keeping some stuff 'hidden', or if you are dating it could mean there may be more you need to learn about the person you are seeing. It is not a negative card unless you have the Seven of Swords or Five of Cups next to it, and then the secrets actually become lies. This is the beauty of card combos. The High Priestess may suggest you wait before making up your mind about something or someone in relation to love, as you do not have all the answers.

Health

You could be always worrying about your health and be constantly Googling. Don't. Just stop. You know your body better than anyone. Trust your intuition and get off the internet.

Card Combinations with the High Priestess

The Hierophant: Could be a school, college, university or place of learning.
Any Pages: Teacher/student
Page of Wands: Psychic reading or psychic reader
The Moon: Intuition is heightened, and you could have revelations or vivid dreams.

Death and The Magician: development of mediumship or spirit trying to connect through the reading.

*If the High Priestess falls beside a Pentacles court card, that means that the person who is appearing in the reading is a Virgo as the High Priestess is governed by Virgo. Through the use of a little Astrology, you can pin point the exact star sign, not just the element.

As an Outcome Card

You could be waiting for answers or needing to have patience. You do not have all the details you need to move forward so you must trust your intuition.

Astrological Association: Virgo

THE EMPRESS

Buzz Words: fertility, abundance, women's rituals, woman's "stuff", creativity, goddess, mother, nurturing, mother earth, Gaia.

THE EMPRESS

General Meaning

When the Empress appears, it does herald fertility, growth and abundance. It can indeed foretell pregnancy or issues around women's fertility and associated issues. It is also a card that talks about comfort, home and security. When appearing in a man's reading it often foretells the love of his life. It can represent a mother or grandmother also. In a woman's reading when this card appears it is also talking about finding your inner goddess and your mojo and sense of self. Creativity and a resurgence of creative impulse to express yourself are also highlighted. Career wise it is often associated with the beauty industry hence its astrological association with Venus.

Finances

When the Empress appears in questions to do with finances it talks about growth and abundance. You could be spending money on pampering yourself or on self- growth or investing in yourself as a means to make money in the future.

Career

The energy of the Empress is one of growth, so if the question is about career direction, the Empress would suggest that the person is about to have a spurt of growth in their career section. Now in itself it will not tell you the career path, but if you read with layering and we will get to that later, you may see someone's life path. If you had the Queen of Cups here, she may be a Nurse or Healer as she is looking after someone empathetically. If the Lovers card fell next to the Empress that would indicate she was creative, perhaps works with color or design, perhaps a makeup artist, hairdresser or an interior decorator. Could also suggest that a woman could be helpful to the person being read for.

Love

The energy of the Empress is the expression of feminine energy. Seeing this card in a love reading means a great time ahead whether married or single. If things have been rocky in your marriage or relationship, you will feel the love again and if single, you will meet someone as a result of loving yourself more, as like attracts like.

Health

This card would relate to a woman's reproductive organs, the womb. Pregnancies, menstrual cycles, menopause, and peri-menopause all fall under the Empress. This card is traditionally the card we look for when people are wanting to fall pregnant and I often see it close to the High Priestess in the early stages.

Card Combinations with the Empress

Ten of Swords: Menstruating or menstrual issues

Five of Cups: Menstrual bleeding

Any Page: Mother-child relationship

Queen of Cups: Midwife

The Lovers: Career in design, color, makeup, wellbeing, artist

The Emperor: Mum and Dad, Grandparents, being in a perfect relationship that would remind you of someone who has been in a long marriage

The Moon: Overly protective, living your life through your children, possessiveness

The Sun: Having children or happiness surrounding children

The Devil: Motherhood getting you down

Death: A passed over female may want to connect from the other side

As an Outcome Card

It is a Yes card as it is positive

Astrological Association: Venus

THE EMPEROR

THE EMPEROR

Buzz Words: boss, authority, structure, stability, solid foundations, power, delegation, calling the shots, business man or woman, doesn't like to be told what to do.

General Meaning

When the Emperor appears in your reading it is talking about structure and the kind of power that arises from it. Could mean a promotion or becoming the "Boss". In career readings it is associated with the Armed Forces, politics, or any job where you are in control, could even be self-employed. The emperor can appear in your reading as a successful business man or woman (look at cards next to it). Can sometimes relate to a father figure or anyone that plays that role in your life. If you are asking a question about your career it might suggest you don't like to be told what to do. In a relationship the Emperor suggests someone that is in control and does not express their emotions freely e.g. "big boys don't cry".

Finances

Taking control of your finances or being self-employed. The word is control. So, if you have had any concerns about your finances it would suggest that you take control over the issues and map out a solid plan to follow as the Emperor is always in control and has a plan. Could also suggest that an older male helps or gives advice regarding a financial concern or how to move forward with a financial plan. You may need to back yourself.

Career

The Emperor is the Boss card, so the energy coming up talks about either being self-employed or a promotion where you are the boss and calling the shots. It is a position of power and delegation. The Emperor can also suggest someone that has your back in an organization that helps you to move forward or helps you to achieve a goal.

Love

The Emperor may describe your partner or your father and the relationship you have with either. It may denote someone coming up if you are single. The Emperor may suggest that you are after more stability or sense of security in your love.

Health

Numerologically related to the number 4, which is structure and solid foundations. Relates to head and headaches (and accidents relating to that part of the body), e.g. if it had the three, or nine of swords around it.

Card Combinations with the Emperor

King of Wands: Is often seen for men in the army
The Sun: Very influential man and most likely a fire sign
Death: Passed over fatherly figure coming through the reading
The Empress: Happy relationship, being on the same page
Ten of Pentacles or Seven of Pentacles: Running your own business

As an Outcome Card

This card is a Yes as it is a solid card, carrying a lot of authority and energy.

Astrological Association: Aries and Mars, so this card holds a lot of energy.

THE HIEROPHANT

Buzz Words: commitment, marriage issues or focus, playing it safe, taking the conservative approach, keeping up with the Jones', government, banks, corporate, structure, learning, religion, following the traditional route, core values

THE HIEROPHANT

General Meaning

Tradition, gateway to hidden knowledge and teachings. When this card comes up, you could be going to university or attend another large institution. This card can also represent someone mentoring you like a priest, friend, relative or someone very conventional. Where the High Priestess is about intuitive insights, the Hierophant is about teachings or learning from a 'structure'.

With the religious overtones, can also mean marriage. This card may appear and does appear for people who like routine and structure. If asking a question and you get this card it is guiding, you to take the conservative approach and not take a risk (unlike the Fool card).

Finances

You could be dealing with banks for loans or credit when the Hierophant appears relating to finances. If you need to make a decision it asks you to take the safe or conservative option. The Hierophant suggests at this time you save the old-fashioned way or just be conservative in any financial decision or investment.

Career

The Hierophant appearing in the career sector would be suggestive of working for a large corporate structure, government department or agency. Perhaps there is an opportunity through a large organisation for you to consider. Security may be important for you in deciding on a new opportunity, so if this card appears it would be suggestive this offer may tick this box for you. If the Justice card appears next to it, you may work for the Police or Justice Department or somewhere with law enforcement or legislation. If the Queen of Cups was near it, you could be working for Community Services.

Love

This is traditionally the marriage and commitment card, so make sure that the cards next to it are not negative as it will take away from the positivity and give it a different meaning. However, if the Hierophant appears in a reading where a person is dating, it suggests that the relationship will develop into something more meaningful or towards further commitment or marriage. If you are in a relationship, you could find your commitment deepening. Your values are what will keep you together, so the Hierophant asks you to consider whether you are both on the same page with what you value in life or what your core values are.

Health

With the Hierophant appearing in health questions, this could relate to hospital or medical tests, especially if followed by the Four of Swords. (It is very important that you do not make any diagnosis in readings as you are not a doctor, so leave it to the professionals.) Sometimes this can show up for people that work in hospitals or visits to hospitals etc.

Card Combinations with the Hierophant

Four of Swords: hospital
Ten of Cups: happy marriage
Six of Pentacles: Working for a non-profit or charity organisation, giving your time to charity

Justice: Taxation Department, Centrelink, government agency

King of Cups: Husband

Queen of Cups: Wife

As an Outcome Card

It is a positive card, so it is a Yes card and the advice is to follow the conservative option.

Astrological Association: Jupiter and the sign Taurus

THE LOVERS

Buzz Words: choices, decisions, values, love coming into your life, soul mates, love connections.

THE LOVERS

General Meaning
Card of love, decisions, unions, choices, soul mates, relationships, values. When this card appears, it could mean harmony in a current relationship and being in alignment with your values. For singles, love will come into your life and there will be instant attraction and a meeting of souls. It is quite powerful, and you may find that you feel that you have known this person for a long time.

Around career, it talks about having to make decisions and choices about your long-term future. Is your career in alignment with your values and home life? If you are reading this as reversed, it would mean you are taking a risk or throwing caution to the wind.

Finances
You could be having to make some major decisions concerning your financial affairs. This could be by accepting a new role or job and having to consider how that affects your finances or what you need to let go of in the process of accepting that offer. There could be two options to consider. You could be investing and there are two options, or you may be looking at two homes and having to decide. Whatever you decide, spirit is

helping you to make the right decision, so do not stress. Everything works out perfectly in divine timing.

Career

You may have two options to consider or to weigh up. Trust your gut instincts for they will not let you down. This is a card about values, so in helping you to decide, are your values in alignment with the company goals or does the job fit in with your home and create the balance that you need? They are all considerations for making a decision when the Lovers card comes up. Sometimes I have seen this pop up when someone meets someone through work. Be careful if it has the Five of Cups next to it, as it will be an affair or fling. As a career, it highlights potential in the beauty industry.

Love

When the Lovers card appears in a love reading you can expect to feel more loving if you are in a relationship, or if you are single, you can expect to meet someone. Now, please note the following: if the Devil card is next to it, it talks about sex or sexual attraction. It could mean that intimacy is an issue or a key to improving the relationship, or if single and you are internet dating, it could mean they are just after sex. Always remember, positive cards against it will amplify the meaning and negative cards will take away from the positivity to some extent, or it will give you a 'buzzword'. So, a lover coming your way if you had the Lovers card with Hierophant could mean someone who wants long term commitment, versus Lovers with the Devil could indicate he or she is after sex or a good time. That may or may not suit you; it just shows you the difference, so you can decide. Is he or she The One (Lovers with Hierophant) or is he or she a Friend with Benefits (Lovers with the Devil)?

Health

The theme of having to make good choices could apply to health if that is an area of concern. Since the Lovers card is to some extent a sexual card, it could denote the sexual organs like the ovaries for a woman etc. Don't get too hung up on it, though. Some tarot readers may get a sense of an issue relating to what we have two of, for example two kidneys, two breasts, because of the duality of this card.

Card Combinations with the Lovers

Two of Cups: Happy relationship, possibly marriage (this goes for Ten of Cups and Ten of Pentacles). If the Ace of Cups was next to it, I would say it is a new relationship

The Devil: Sexual attraction and perhaps sex is a focus or need. Someone only wanting sex

Five of Cups: Betrayal. I often see this for affairs or other issues with relationships

Five of Cups and Three of Cups: Swingers or open relationship, or a player

The Empress: Being the love of someone's life, beauty and creativity

Five of Wands/Swords: arguments with someone you love

Strength: Someone highly creative that works with design, is a good manager or able to plan events

As an Outcome Card

It is a positive card. As a Yes/No, it comes down to your choice, but it is favorable. You are making the right decision.

Astrological Association

Gemini, hence the duality and needing to make choices. Look at the card - there are two lovers, e.g. Adam and Eve. There is also an element of swords here, which is about communication.

THE CHARIOT

Buzz Words: taking control, overcoming obstacles, forging ahead, travel, cars, journeys, feeling back in control over your life

THE CHARIOT

General Meaning

When the Chariot appears in your reading, it tells you that you are in the driver's seat and you can take control over your destiny. Any obstacles will be overcome, and victory is yours. Achieving your goals and worldly pursuits are now possible; keep forging ahead. You will have the tools and resources necessary to achieve what you set out to do. The Chariot also predicts journeys and cars.

Finances

Overcoming difficulties around finances or feeling like you are on top of your bills. It's under control. With the Chariot appearing for finances, money could be going out on a vehicle or travelling. If a new car, you will see the Ace of Wands next to it. If issues around a car, you will probably find the Five of Pentacles close by (money going out). If you are reading with singular cards, just take the basic meaning for now - you can grow your vocabulary later. It means gaining control of your finances.

Career

Making a career move could be what you need when the Chariot appears. You may want to move forward. If there have been issues, it talks about getting your sense of control back or feeling in control again. When this card appears in the career section, you could also be travelling with your job. If it has the Six of Swords next to it, it could be an interstate trip or with the World, could be overseas. The Chariot heralds success on the career front, but you need to take control of the reigns again and follow through on your decision making.

Love

The theme is overcoming obstacles if in love. It's not an overly emotional nor a love card as such, but it is suggestive of perhaps keeping your emotions in check and knowing that you can overcome issues if you are in a relationship. If you are looking for love, it would suggest not to give up as you will find it. Perhaps you need to travel to meet someone or leave the house? The Chariot could describe someone who works in logistics or with cars as a potential person coming into your life, so you recognise him or her when they appear.

Health

Overcoming issues and feeling back in control of your life and wellbeing. You are on the home stretch so don't give up now. Hurdles will be overcome.

Card Combinations with the Chariot

The Star: Overcoming health issues

King of Swords: Someone who works with cars

Two of Pentacles: Shipping and logistics

Eight of Wands: A focus on travel could even mean a job where a lot of driving is required

As an Outcome Card

A success and victory card, so a Yes card.

Astrological Association: Cancer

STRENGTH

Buzz Words: patience, strength, courage, resolution, kindness, pets, animals, forgiveness, managers, energy, improvement around health

STRENGTH

General Meaning

When this card appears in a reading, it is talking about finding the strength to overcome any obstacles and having the courage and conviction to do it. Also, if you are asking whether you will resolve differences, this is a yes! The image portrays a figure patting a pet, and sometimes this does translate to a real pet. It is an energy card, so if a person is unwell, it advises you that they will regain their strength and things will improve but remember to look at surrounding cards. It is also a card about having to have patience and that things may take time. You may need to manage people when this card appears, so sometimes it also has an association with managers.

Finances

Patience is required or perhaps having to save for some financial goal or desire. It is not about giving up, but about being realistic about the timeframe. It is about managing your money properly and knowing that it takes time for things to come together. The key word is managing your money wisely - no get rich quick schemes.

Career

This card often comes up for managers or managerial positions in a career reading. You may need to have some patience about career goals. If this card appears and you want to throw in your job, you are asked to have some patience as things will improve. Unless there are other cards that diminish the meaning, for example, if the Hanged Man was next to it, perhaps all the patience in the world is never going to change as circumstances may be out of your control. However, if the Strength card was with the Nine of Wands, it would be advising you not to throw in the towel - that you have put in so much effort and come so far - and to have a little more patience that things will improve.

Love

This card is about kindness and forgiveness, so you may need to forgive someone that is close to you. You may need to practice patience in a relationship as your loved one is stressed, or you may need to forgive and let go to move forward. If you are single, do you need to forgive someone from the past or cut an energy cord, so you can invite new love in? You may find when this card appears, you attract kind people into your life that show that they care.

Health

The Strength Card is primarily an energy card - look at the vibrant colours - so if your health has been a concern, it talks about an increase in vitality. It is also suggestive of taking more vitamins and being gentle with yourself in optimizing your health. Animals could help you to relax, thus helping your overall health.

Card Combinations with Strength

The Star: good or improved health

Ten of Swords/Wands: you may be feeling very run down

King of Swords: chiropractors, naturopaths or alternate health therapists

Page of Cups: a baby animal or pet

The Lovers: a very creative person who may work with design, colour or art

As an Outcome Card

The Strength card is a positive card, so it is a Yes card, but patience will be needed, or a waiting period required before you may see results.

Astrological Association: Leo

THE HERMIT

THE HERMIT

Buzz Words: meditation, guidance, inner wisdom, feeling alone, withdrawal from the world, introspection, reflection, working by yourself

General Meaning

When this card appears, it guides you to go within for the answers - away from the world. Introspection, inner guidance, and reflection are key words for this card. Also, it asks you to keep your counsel and be mindful to keep things close to your chest at this point in time. It can also indicate a person coming into your life that will guide, mentor or teach you. It is often a wise person.

Finances

You may be seeking advice regarding your finances, but you are also asked to go with what you are feeling about a matter as you know yourself best. Know that the decisions you are making are wise and that you have thought a lot about future plans that involve money or investments. If you are feeling uncertain, then this card would be suggestive of seeking guidance.

Career

You may be working alone or having to drive yourself with your career or work. When this card appears, you may be seeking answers about your life path or what you should be doing, and you are asked to go within to hear the answers. Careers in meditation or mediation are governed by this card, as well as teaching.

Love

You may be feeling alone even if you are in a relationship or wanting some space if this card appears in a love reading. Or, you may be spending time by yourself as part of your job and this may be making you feel a little lonely. Perhaps this time of being alone is healing the emotions within you that need to be healed, so don't be in a hurry. Use this time for self-love and healing. There is plenty of time to reconnect with others. You need to fill your own cup first.

Health

Meditation, Pilates or yoga may help to de-stress you or help with anxiety. You may need to look within to help you with your health concerns, and a mind over matter approach will be beneficial. Taking more vitamins and being gentle with yourself in optimizing your health may also be a good idea.

Card Combinations with The Hermit

The Hierophant: a traditional teacher or mentor e.g. school teacher or priest
The High Priestess: a spiritual teacher or someone experienced with intuition
King of Swords: psychologist (mind, thoughts -swords)
Any court card: teacher/student relationship

As an Outcome Card

The Hermit is a wisdom card, so it is a positive card as an outcome.

Astrological Association: Virgo

WHEEL OF FORTUNE

Buzz Words: change for the better, luck, good fortune, advancement, karmic change, lady luck

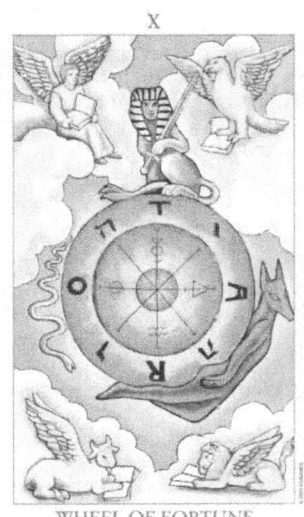
WHEEL OF FORTUNE

General Meaning
When the Wheel of Fortune appears, the tide is turning and new events and favourable changes are about to occur. If you are hoping for something to happen, or you are waiting for a result, luck is on your side. The Wheel of Fortune is also about cyclic change – if you have had a really rough time, this is what you are looking for to instill renewed hope that things are going to get better. If you are looking for a job, you would have a good chance of getting it if this card appears in the reading, or if you are waiting on some outcome it will be favourable.

Finances
Luck may play a part in getting ahead financially. Something exciting or an offer may come your way that helps your financial situation. When the Wheel of Fortune falls in your money sector, you can expect positive change, be it through something that makes you feel lucky or that you were not expecting. It could be a win or gift, or something a little left field. In any case, count your blessings, financial improvement is on its way.

Career
Right place, right time sort of energy when this card appears in your career section. You could be given a lucky break, or some fantastic opportunity comes up. You may need

to say 'yes' and work out the finer details later. Always double check surrounding cards, and that they are positive (I am a Virgo admittedly, but I do like to see positive cards next to the Wheel of Fortune, too). You can expect positive change when you see this card appearing and you may need to pinch yourself.

Love

If you are married, it doesn't mean you are going to change your partner, it just means that your relationship strengthens or changes favourably – you may be feeling lucky to have your partner in your life. If you are single, you may have the opportunity to meet someone new. The Wheel appearing in the love sector would show a shift in your circumstances for the better - Lady Luck is coming to help you on this front, so know that your status or circumstances are going to change.

Health

Improvements around health or making positive changes to your health are indicated. If you are worried about something, the results are better than expected.

Card Combinations with The Wheel of Fortune

Ace of Pentacles: a monetary win

Ten of Swords (or any negative cards): the upcoming change has challenges

Positive cards: enhances and gives you detail of the change e.g. The Lovers indicates a love life back on track

As an Outcome Card

It is an extremely positive and lucky card, so this is a Yes card, denoting favourable outcomes and circumstances.

Astrological Association: Jupiter – planet of luck and expansion.

JUSTICE

Buzz Words: legal matters or advice/ official documentation, contracts, decisions, departments, law enforcement

JUSTICE

General Meaning

When this card appears, it often talks about legal issues, contracts, and decisions. It's the card of 'reap what you sow' in outcomes, so it is talking about fairness, arbitration and settlements. The cards that fall beside it will determine its meaning, however in itself, it is about fairness and issues being favourable if you have done the right thing.

Finances

Decisions around money matters, obtaining legal advice, perhaps with settlements, wills or estates. Since this card also rules official paperwork, you may need to deal with red tape or with large organisations, such as superannuation or claims etc. Always look at surrounding cards to see if they're favourable. Legal advice may be the answer or the key to solving some issue that perhaps cannot be resolved another way.

Career

The Justice card is a very organisational card, and I often see it for corporate or government bodies, insurance companies etc. If there are a lot of swords appearing next to it, for e.g. the Eight of Swords, the person could be associated with correctional services, police, law, criminology or legislation etc. In any case, the basic meaning is about decisions that are work related. If this card is afflicted and it has the Seven of

Swords, Five of Swords or Five of Cups with it, you or someone you are reading for could be suffering from some *injustice*. Blending the cards will give you more meaning but for now, if the Justice card appears in the career section, the subject of what is fair could be an issue. You may be weighing up options in order to make a decision about your plans moving forward.

Love

The Justice card is a very detached and unemotional card and it may mean you are seeking legal advice about your financial status with a partner. This does not always point to divorce, unless other cards are suggestive of that. It could also mean changing name and dealing with official paperwork. If you are single, you may be looking at your options, but it is a very unemotional card; the sparks may not be there. If it is around a court card, it may describe a person that is divorced, so if they show up you will know who it is. It may describe the occupation that a potential love interest is involved in, or if they have legal dealings going on in their life.

Health

The Justice card in health readings always talks about the battle of the scales and if positively aspected, it shows success around weight goals. Weighing food or scales are buzzwords in health, so weight could be an issue for other health related issues. Now, please be mindful how you use this in a reading as it is a sore point for many of us. I would say that health and wellbeing is a focus with nutrition being the key to optimum health. There are positive ways to deliver messages.

Card Combinations with Justice

Ace of Swords: clarity, resolution, contracts, divorce if it is coupled with the Devil or Death card

The Hierophant: coming together through marriage, government departments e.g. justice with the justice department or the police force

The Emperor: a judge or someone that upholds the law

The High Priestess and King of Swords: undercover detective

Eight of Swords: imprisonment or being imprisoned with your own limiting thoughts

Two of Cups: legalizing a partnership

Five of Swords: litigation

Five of Pentacles: legal losses

Any King: father in law or stepfather

Court card and Death: an in-law or step parent in spirit coming through reading

Six of Pentacles: settlement (favourable)

Ten of Pentacles: estate, wills and inheritances

As an Outcome Card

The Justice card is a favourable card and a Yes Card

Astrological Association: Libra

THE HANGED MAN

Buzz Words: sacrifice, suspension, waiting, martyrdom, life on hold, humanitarianism

THE HANGED MAN

General Meaning

When this card shows up, you may find that you are unable to move forward and that there are outside forces at work. Other people may be preventing you from making changes to your life and decisions could involve other people. Your life may be on hold, or the feeling that it is never changing when the Hanged Man appears. Sometimes it can be through circumstances out of your control. The lesson is to surrender and not fight against it. Things will change, or events will happen when they are supposed to, and not one minute before.

Finances

There could be something stemming from your past that could be a block with regards to getting ahead financially or matters to do with credit. This could relate to financial mistakes or costly financial decisions that could still be a cloud over your head. Know that it won't last forever, however, the Hanged Man's energy does sit around for a while. Do some research: there are always solutions to problems, but you may need to keep looking.

Career

When the Hanged Man appears in the career sector, you may feel like you are working extremely hard and not making much headway. You may be waiting for that promotion or for an increase, but there is no new opportunity coming your way. Look at surrounding cards following this. Are they positive to suggest that you will overcome this stagnant stage, or is it followed by more pain - especially if you have Sword cards close by (e.g. Ten of Swords etc.)? You may be doing humanitarian work as this is a card of sacrifice and helping mankind. This is a card of waiting and suspension, and often I see it when there is no movement or change to status quo.

Love

When this card appears in love, you may lose your sense of self in relationship, you may give up your ideals for another person, or the relationship could become enmeshed. There is a lesson of having to put one's self-first, as the word that is conjured here is 'martyrdom'. If you are single, there might be issues to do with commitment, not wanting to take things to the next level, creating uncertainty or issues around security.

Health

Putting others before your own needs could be an issue with your health goals and concerns. No change to status quo. If weight loss concerns you, you may be on a plateau.

Card Combinations with The Hanged Man

Two of Cups (or any relationship cards): may suggest relationship is not moving forward or you're losing yourself within the relationship

Death: a really slow transformation or ending. On a positive note, there will be an end to something that has dragged on

Strength: needing to draw on your inner strength and resilience to keep going

Six of Pentacles: working for charity

As an Outcome Card

The energy of the Hanged Man is one of waiting for something to happen, or you will be waiting a long time for the result you are wanting. While it's not a negative card, I do not consider it a Yes card, only because what you are wanting seems too far away to be in reach when this card comes up.

Astrological Association: Pisces

DEATH

Buzz words: endings, transformation, time to let go of the past and move on, always look towards surrounding cards or positions for more information to show you where the end or change takes place.

DEATH

General Meaning

So, we come to the most terrifying card of the deck. It always shows us an ending but promises us a new beginning. Endings are never easy as we as humans at times find it difficult to deal with changes and the deep-rooted emotions when dealing with this.

There is no doubt this is a difficult card, but it does promise a new beginning and new prospects. It rarely relates to physical death. Morally and ethically, you should not ever bring up a death to someone. They are coming to you to give them guidance, encouragement and the possibilities that are presented within the reading. They are not coming to you to predict a death. At times, they may ask if they have a relative that is very ill, but that is still a matter for God, not for us mere mortals to give a time frame. If they know their loved one is passing, it goes without saying that they should spend more time with them or heal any emotional rifts if possible.

Finances

You may need to make some big changes to your finances or there are changes coming. This sometimes comes up in conjunction with changes in the career sector that may affect your finances. Change is good - it brings growth - so do not be scared if this appears; there is another opportunity coming your way even if something does come to an end. Sometimes this may come up if you are refinancing or changing your finances in some way. The word you are going to grab is "change" or "end" and apply it to your financial situation, or for the person you are reading for. Sometimes the Death card is something we are wanting in our lives to change the status quo. If we have been having difficulty with our finances and the Death card appears, that may be a blessing that things will change. If there were negative cards nearby such as the Tower and the Five of Pentacles, you would suggest that the person go and see a financial advisor or someone that could assist with a debt arrangement. The Death card is a very transformative card so when it shows up, the person will learn a lot of financial lessons that will help them in the future.

Career
Big change. Something comes to an end. Career change or change of direction.

Love
The Death card around love readings can indicate major changes or indeed, endings. It could relate to big events that affect relationships, however not necessarily between the people involved. It is important to look at surrounding cards to see the energy at play. This card is not a positive card unless you are indeed wanting big changes.

Health
Do not stress. It does *not* mean death. If you are reading for a woman, it could mean change of life, it could mean changing doctors or diet. It may mean having to change some current practice in order to bring about a change for the better. If the Star should show up next to it, someone may indeed have mental health issues, so the message is to ask, "are you okay?"

Card Combinations with Death
Ace of Wands: rebirth
The Moon and The Magician, and possibly a court card: there is someone trying to connect from the other side

Page of Cups: miscarried babies or children from the other side

The Hierophant and Four of Wands: funeral home (could be someone's occupation)

Ace of Cups: relationship ending in its current form, but starting again afresh

Three of Swords: challenging time

Ten of Pentacles: strengthens inheritance interpretation

The Hermit and King of Swords: counselling for grief

The Fool: going in a totally new direction

As an Outcome Card

As this card is considered a negative card, it is a No card.

Astrological Association: Scorpio

TEMPERANCE

Buzz words: healing, balance, reconciliation, moderation, patience, ability to manage, administrator

General Meaning

When the Temperance card appears, we need to create balance in our lives or take a balanced approach in all matters. The word 'healing' comes alive when this card appears, so if there has been any imbalance, disputes or unrest in your life, restoration, harmony or peace will occur.

Finances

As it is a card of balance, you may need to watch your accounts more carefully and take a more moderate approach to spending. If you have financial issues, the Temperance card would suggest that you can sort any concerns out through careful management of your funds.

Career

This is the 'administrators' card. If this card turns up for a career reading, one must be objective or take a middle ground approach. If there has been some competition or strife around a work situation, you may find it will be sorted out through some form of mediation.

Love

If there has been disputes around emotional matters, wounds can be healed, and reconciliation can occur. You may need to compromise to move forward from matters that are challenging relationships and accept other people's point of view and feelings.

Card Combinations with Temperance

Justice: favourable litigation outcomes

Ace of Swords: breakthrough in negotiations

Queen of Cups: a nurse or healer

King of Swords: a doctor

King of Cups and Strength: alternative healer, e.g. a chiropractor

As an Outcome Card

The Temperance Card is a positive card, so it is a Yes Card.

Astrological Association: Sagittarius

THE DEVIL

Buzz Words: Feeling trapped, materialism, sex, bondage, frustration, restriction, depression

THE DEVIL

General Meaning

Burden of materialism, desire for physical and material things, feelings of frustration and repression. You are driven by your basic instincts. You need to take responsibility for your actions. This card could sometimes indicate a preoccupation with materialism and a reluctance to change in this area, which can come at the expense of growth. Addictions also come under this card.

Finances

Finances maybe tight. You may be feeling overwhelmed by your financial responsibilities or going through a period where finances are a concern or a focus.

Career

Wanting change, however feeling trapped due to financial obligations and the money that your current career may bring. There is an internal struggle with desire and entrapment.

Love

Falling in a love reading, the Devil card would be suggestive of sexual matters as being a key issue or problem. The Devil card also suggests that within a relationship, someone is suffering from depression and that would be affecting the relationship. It is a difficult card when it falls in the relationship sector, and you should look at surrounding cards for further clarification on how one can push through the difficulties.

Health

As a health concern, The Devil can represent depression or addiction. Be careful not to diagnose though, unless you are a qualified health professional. It can suggest that the person that the reading relates to could possibly benefit from counselling.

Card Combinations with The Devil

Seven of Swords: anxiety

King of Cups and Three of Cups: someone addicted to alcohol or drugs, a depressed man

The Hermit: lonely and reclusive. Need to get out more

The Lovers and Three of Cups: addicted to sex

Four of Pentacles: hugely materialistic

Three of Wands: opportunistic (not in a good way)

The Moon: moody, nightmares

Strength: lack of energy or unwell

Queen of Swords: bitchy

Nine of Cups: weight gain

Tower or Death: always give further strength to this card in a negative way

Five of Wands or Swords: arguments get out of hand

The Magician: you are dealing with a narcissist

As an Outcome Card

Negative card, negative outcome. It is a No card.

Astrological Association: Capricorn and Saturn. Key words: restrictive, responsibility

THE TOWER

THE TOWER

Buzz words: sudden change, feeling shocked, foundations rocked, big moves, revelations

General Meaning

Sweeping change that may rock your foundations. Sudden revelations often come as a shock. Despite the disruption, change happens in your life as your circumstances were built on shaky grounds. The changes often bring freedom and deeper enlightenment and awareness.

Finances

The finance and career sectors are always closely linked, so one affects the other. If the person isn't working, it could mean that there are changes to their financial affairs. It is important to see what is next to the Tower. I do not see this as a negative card in itself, as the change can be lucky if it has positive cards nearby. If, however it has negative cards such as the Five of Pentacles, it could mean bankruptcy or financial debt.

Career

If the Tower appears in the career sector with the Five of Pentacles, there could be unexpected job loss, restructures and so forth. It does denote big change, though. Look at the surrounding cards; if it has court cards around it, someone might be leaving. If the Emperor is there, it could be your boss. If you are self-employed you may need to make some big changes in order to grow your business. Something unexpected could happen that could affect your career.

Health

The suddenness of the Tower could sometimes mean the onset of a change in someone's life, e.g., menopause. It is traditionally associated with accidents, etc., in the old tarot books, but again it would have to have a series of negative cards to suggest it, and it is certainly not helpful to relay this sort of information anyway. High blood pressure and headaches come under Mars and the Tower.

Love

The tower can spark arguments in relationships or things happen unexpectedly. You may feel shocked at revelations. You may even question the person in your life and ask, 'Who are you?' If single, things may change.

Card Combinations with The Tower

Death: major changes and transformations, difficult times

Three of Swords: sudden tears and emotional situations

Wheel of Fortune: change for the better, turn of events that are positive

Five of Pentacles: bankruptcy, financial loss

Five of Cups: great disappointment and bewilderment

The World or Four of Wands: house move

Six of Cups: seeing/hearing from someone from your past unexpectedly

The Lovers: unexpected love coming

Wheel of Fortune and Ace of Pentacles: a win

When the Tower appears before another card. it often foretells something unexpected.

As an Outcome Card

The Tower is a card of change and it's important to see what is next to it to see if it's positive or negative.

Astrological Association: Mars

THE STAR

Buzz words: trust, hope, renewed faith and hope for the future, health, good health

THE STAR

General Meaning

When this card appears in your reading, you will have renewed faith and hope for the future. Negativity will be discarded, and you will have more spiritual insights and clarity. It also is a card of healing - both physically and mentally. It's a card of trust.

Finances

The Star, being a positive card, gives hope to financial matters and brings blessings. It may also suggest investing in your health. Finances will improve when the Star appears, as it is a message of hope and restoration.

Career

This card rules health and wellbeing industries. Renewal of direction in the career sector is amplified when the Star card appears. If there has been despondency over progress, the Star card reassures one to keep positive and to trust that it will all align at the right time, or that a new job is on the horizon.

Health

The Star falling for a health question denotes restoration or good health. You will find that the Star falling either in a health reading or in an astrology reading in the health house, will be a big focus for the person being read.

Love

Trust issues or concerns may come up in a relationship reading. If the Star had the Seven of Swords next to it, the concerns are more likely associated with 'mistrust'. This could cause angst in a relationship. If the Star is describing someone you are with or are asking about, the person is trustworthy. If the relationship has been rocky, The Star comforts us and lets us know that we can work through the issues with open communication and being honest. The Star is all about honesty and integrity.

Card Combinations with The Star

Four of Swords: healing after being unwell

Death: life and death, but often talks about drama, could also mean people working in emergency situations. I often see this combination in readings for people who have felt suicidal or someone in their lives has, and this has had a lot of impact on them

Seven of Swords: untrustworthy

The Moon: intuitive counsellor

The High Priestess: psychic healing, healer, spiritual teacher

As an Outcome Card

It is the most positive card in the deck, so it is a big Yes card.

Astrological Association: Aquarius

THE MOON

THE MOON

Buzz words: water, tears, confusion, lack of clarity, mind games, lies, emotions, counselling, psychic ability, trust your gut, dreams, revelations or messages from spiritual realms

General Meaning

The Moon relates to your subconscious, psychic impressions, revelations through dreams and illusion. The Moon can represent occupations such as entertainment, drama, television, media, psychic counselling or subconscious work. The Moon will appear when you are emotional - you may not understand what is driving this emotional state - there is this heightened sensitivity to all energy as things and people around you are not transparent, or they may be playing mind games with you. Can sometimes indicate confusion.

Finances

Watch out for scams when the Moon card falls in a finance reading or read the fine print. It is a card of financial confusion, misinformation or lack of clarity, and the advice is not to move forward on anything while this vibe or energy is around. Obtain more information or trust your gut instincts before moving forward. This warns you not to go through with things unless you check details.

Career

This card covers counsellors as a vocation. In a career reading, this could be suggestive of jealousy and competition and the advice is not to feed it. Look at the cards around it - if you have court cards or if The World was next to it, you may have someone in the public eye/media/actor etc., as the World governs public acclaim. The Moon in the career sector at first glance would tell me this is an area where you may be feeling vulnerable, and it could be because you are comparing yourself, or there is jealousy or some toxicity within the work environment that you need to detach from. There could be a lack of clarity and direction when the Moon appears, so it is suggestive of finding out more information or allowing time to pass before making any decisions.

Health

Nutrition and detoxing could be beneficial, as well as increasing water consumption. The Moon governs emotions, so counselling could also assist with wellbeing. The Moon is also associated with cycles, so could point to issues with women's monthly cycles as well as hormone fluctuations.

Love

Could someone in your life be keeping secrets from you? The Moon shows that someone is not telling you everything there is to tell or playing mind games. It's not in your head – if you are picking up intuitively that someone is not telling you the truth, you will be on the money. Just remember that all secrets are found out and revelations will follow, so tears often accompany the Moon for that reason.

Card Combinations with The Moon

The Devil: jealousy, addictive behaviours including drinking, drugs etc., as this is an outlet for unresolved feelings, depression and moodiness

Seven of Swords: lies and deceit, someone not being transparent

Death: mediumship, connecting with spirit

Page of Cups: psychic gut feelings

The Tower: emotional upheaval

The High Priestess: psychically gifted empath

The Magician: someone who can really read and manipulate people. Can be positive or negative

Temperance: spiritual healer

Ace of Swords: emotional clarity

Three of Swords: tears and emotionally draining times

The World: entertainment industry, someone in the limelight

Three of Pentacles: a restaurant or theatre, somewhere with dim lights and ambience.

Five of Cups: lovers, and with the Three of Cups and Three of Pentacles – a brothel!

As an Outcome Card

As outcome card, the Moon can be a dodgy card. It's probably not what you are after and it gets a No from me. It has elements of dishonesty or illusion, so if you compare it to the Star of honesty and hope, you can see what I'm saying.

Astrological Association: Cancer and Pisces

THE SUN

Buzz words: Happiness joy, vitality prosperity good health, growth, promotions, success, children, abundance, happiness

THE SUN

General Meaning
When you draw this card, just know that better times are ahead of you. The Sun will shine on you - literally. It always heralds positivity.

Career
Expect to shine when the Sun appears. It is your time. If you have been looking for a job, expect to get it. If you are up for a promotion, chances are you will succeed. There is a lot of power in the Sun. It holds a lot of positive and uplifting energy, so take advantage of offers coming your way, as you do not know where it may lead. If you have been feeling tested, the Sun reassures you things will change positively for you, so do not give up. If things have been good, they are going to get better. Success and happy outcomes are to be expected. As a career, this card is associated with working with children.

Finances
Money matters improve. It suggests positive outcomes such increased savings or being able to save, getting return on investments or profiting from a venture.

Love

Feeling more optimistic and confident about love, romance and relationships. This can also indicate improved relationships around children. If you have had tears, The Sun gently wipes them away and restores your faith in love. Your heart is full again.

Health

Increased vitality is suggested with the Sun appearing in a health reading. The Sun appearing suggests recovery from illness or being able to transcend bouts of depression. I will say this over and over during this book that unless you are a health professional, do not make a diagnosis - this is simply a tool of exploration and self-development.

Card Combinations with The Sun

The Empress: creativity, children are highlighted
The Emperor: a man involved is a Leo.
The Lovers (or any positive cup cards): enhances a close and loving relationship
Any court card: that person is a positive influence
Three of Swords, Death or Ten of Swords: heart problems
Pages: happy children, working with children
The Hierophant: happy marriage
The World: great accomplishment
Whichever card the Sun is next to, it makes it more positive. This card is a meaning in itself.

As an Outcome Card

The Sun card holds so much energy, that you can only expect positive outcomes. It is a Yes card.

Astrological associations: Leo, Sun

JUDGEMENT

Buzz words: Life review, clear thinking, re-evaluation, re-birth, spiritual awakening, renewal, career move, judging, discernment, needing to make decisions, resurrection

JUDGEMENT

General Meaning

This card appears when we are at a cross road in our lives. It is a time to let go of what is not working in one's life in order to bring in more balance and enlightenment. You may feel like walking away from situations that no longer hold appeal. Judgement can indicate renewed health (look towards surrounding cards or positional meanings). I call this stripping back the layers to work out if something is working for you or not. A time to move on from the limitations of the past and move forward in making decisions.

Career

Cross road time. Your career may no longer hold appeal. You have learnt all there is to learn, or you have outgrown it. It's time to make some decisions about the future and weigh up your options. Decisions are favourable if the Judgement card is favourably aspected with positive cards surrounding it. Someone may want to retire or bring in more life/work balance as a reason to make changes to their working life.

Love

Judgement can sometimes mean plain old *judgement*. Is someone being too judgmental in a relationship? Are the cons outweighing the pros regarding staying in a relationship? This is a card about reviewing one's life and in context to relationships, you may be weighing up your options.

Health

This is a card about doing a health review or having a check-up. Your lifestyle may be out of balance and you are needing to let go of routines or practices that are not supportive to your health.

Card Combinations with Judgement

Five of Cups: dealing with unresolved issues from the past. Learning not to live in the past in order to move forward

Strength: rebirth and resurgence of creativity

Death: transformation, but through serious life lessons (out of your control)

Eight of Swords: procrastination

The Emperor and Justice: a judge may be deciding any legal issue

I always find this is a very transitional card that it shows an ending and a new beginning. It's a card that I often re read the meaning, as during your tarot journey your interpretations can change.

As an Outcome Card

It is a positive card and a Yes card. Judgements will be made in your favour.

Astrological influence: Moon

THE WORLD

THE WORLD

Buzz words: Success, accomplishments, attainment, onwards and upwards, change of residence, overseas travel, completion of personal cycle, culmination of events, something coming to fruition, new places, new faces

General Meaning

When the World appears, we feel successful or we are proud that we have achieved goals or completed cycles in our lives. The World card heralds travelling overseas and experiencing new cultures or meeting new people. The World promises success and accomplishment in whatever you do, so it is a wonderful card to draw, especially as an outcome card.

Career

This card is always about being in the public eye, so you may be dealing with the public. It heralds success and acclaim, especially if you have the Moon or Magician nearby. There is a sense of accomplishing goals or perhaps achieving KPI's. You may be required to travel overseas with your job or there could be an overseas connection with upcoming opportunities. If you have worried whether a job or path will be successful, this is the card of accomplishment.

Finances

Since this card is about closing off cycles, you might be able to close off old debt or achieve some financial goal. Money could be spent on going overseas. You could be focusing on saving money to move to a new house or buy a home, as this card is about moves. Since it is a positive card, you can expect finances to be positive coming up in relation to any questions asked.

Love

Love and travelling could go hand in hand. You may be travelling with your significant other, or if you are single, you may meet someone while overseas or with someone that has an overseas connection. It would be a good time to get out and meet new people and even new cultures, as you do not know who you will meet.

Health

Successful completion of health and/or wellbeing goals.

Card Combinations with the World

Eight of Wands: overseas air travel

Knight of Wands: house move

Queen of Swords: a worldly, self-assured woman

Eight of Pentacles: event management course

Nine of Pentacles: sunny overseas destination

Six of Swords: travel around water

The Chariot and Two of Pentacles: cruise overseas

The Moon: acting, theatre, having a public audience

Page of Wands: getting a book published (also any images with scrolls, like High Priestess)

The Chariot: you've got the world at your feet and you are in control

Three of Wands and Two of Pentacles: importing and exporting

As an Outcome Card

The World is a card of huge success and accomplishment and this is a big Yes card.

Astrological association: Saturn

COURT CARDS

Court Cards Overview

The four court cards - Page, Knight, Queen and King usually represent people in your everyday life. They also have abstract meanings which may include positive or negative aspects of your personality. Most of the time in a reading, they will represent a person or news of a person.

The court cards that appear in a reading will generally be people that are in your life and will describe situations that play out and how you may react in relation to these events. What falls besides the court cards will tell you more about the people and the energy you are dealing with. If the Seven of Swords was beside the King of Swords for example, you would be warned not to trust a male in your life or to question the authenticity of a matter. On the other hand, if you had the Three of Wands next to the King of Swords, an opportunity may come through a male contact. So, it is important to read cards in context to other cards to give you 'buzzwords' or card combo meanings.

Whilst the court cards may have ages and physical descriptions associated with them, I would not get hung up on them, as they are not always accurate unless you have other cards that may reinforce these attributes. Refer to my table that summarizes the key words and star sign association. The most important thing to remember is your intent behind the court card, e.g. will you define people by star sign or colouring? Remember that choosing the intent before you read will help the accuracy.

Choosing a Significator
A significator is a card chosen to represent the client or person being asked about in a reading. We often use either a court card that would represent a person's age, colouring, gender or astrological sign. I have found over the years that the astrological sign has had far greater accuracy. However, remember whatever meaning you give to a card or the

intention you give it will be accurate for you. You can also choose some major arcana cards such as the Emperor to represent a father figure or Empress a mother. Significators are optional; however, I have found that by using them as a focal point I can easily tune into anyone. This is particularly helpful when you are doing a reading where a mother has lots of children, for example.

Kings

All four Kings represent dynamic energy. They symbolize power. They can appear in life as male authority or father figures. They will represent older males.

Queens

The Queens represent the power of femininity. They often appear in your life as motherly figures or women that may be related to you. They will represent older females. Traditionally the Queens will represent women over thirty, however don't get too hung up on ages.

Knights

Knights express the extreme of the suits quality. They have an immature attitude and represent the best and worst of the suit's energy. For example, the Knight of Swords rushes into making a decision without thinking about the consequences, and the Knight of Wands may be charming, but totally insensitive. The King on the other hand, knows through life experience what to say or what not to say due to his age. The Knights represent younger men.

Pages

Pages have a light-hearted energy due to association with children or younger people. They represent the playful spirit of the energy of the suit and the child within you. Pages appear in readings as children or younger people. They also represent messengers or messages you will receive. The pages in the tarot do not have a sex attached to them. They represent a younger person or child.

PAGE OF CUPS

Buzz words: Increased intuition, birth of child, gut feelings, happy emotional message, water sign

Abstract buzz words: Awareness and Emotion (when we are not relating the card to a person, but as an abstract meaning

General Meaning
When the Page of Cups stands for a person, it signifies a gentle, imaginative child or adolescent who is sensitive and loving. The Page of Cups as an abstract meaning often appears when we receive some happy emotional news. All the pages are messengers. Look at the suit of Pages as to what the message may be about.

As an abstract card, it can mean the dawning of creativity, intuitive impulses or gut feelings. These are likely to expressed through dreams, reading or talking about spiritual subjects. This Page is often the deliverer of some happy emotional news.

Finances
Good news to lift your spirits concerning your finances. You may want to follow your gut instincts with decision making. Money could be going out on a child's needs. A child or student could be a solution for a financial gain or outcome (e.g. homing overseas students).

Career
You may hear some good news about developments around work. You need to trust your gut instincts at this time to follow leads or ideas, as they will be beneficial for career prospects.

If the Hermit is next to the Page, it could signify a teacher or training role. You may need to further your education to build your resume.

Love

Children may be a focus within a relationship. A child may be needing your attention right now. You may have renewed feelings for your partner. Should there be negative cards surrounding this, it could mean that there is childishness at play within the relationship.

Health

Cups are to do with our emotions, so your emotional health might be a focus. You may need to trust your gut instincts about your health and wellbeing at this time and follow through any concerns that you have. Drinking more water could be helpful.

Card Combinations with Page of Cups

The Empress: happy news of a pregnancy, creative new beginning
The Moon: heightened psychic ability, vivid dreams
The Hermit: teacher/student relationship however this applies to all of the pages The Moon and The Devil: nightmares for children
Ace of Swords: birth of baby girl
Ace of Wands: birth of baby boy

As an Outcome Card

You will be able to foretell the outcome using your intuition. The Page of Cups always heralds positive news.

KNIGHT OF CUPS

Buzz words: Love entering your life, dreams, ideals, opportunity coming your way, water sign
Abstract buzz words: Developing creativity and spirituality

General Meaning

The Knight of Cups is sometimes linked to the legendary Grail Knight who rides off in search of an enlightened ideal. He most often signifies that a lover is on his way or has just entered someone's life. Here, love is elevated and romantic - reality and familiarity have yet to intrude upon this shining dream 'honeymoon stage'. When indicating a person, this Knight is usually a spiritual, emotional young man; a 'metro sexual'. He is sensitive, artistic or musical and has high ideals. Negatively aspected, this Knight has emotional issue and lacks motivation. He is often seeking advice, but not following any. He is likely to be lazy and would rather sleep and read, rather than to act and find. His fantasies do not live up to reality.

As an abstract meaning, this Knight stands for blossoming creativity and an interest in spiritual concerns. It can refer to classes, yoga, psychic development and meditation. If this card has the Devil beside it, it can stand for drugs/dealers, relationships are not what they seem, or a lover is leaving.

Finances
New opportunity or new ways to create more income. This could be linked to the career sector, so always read in conjunction with one another. If finances have been

tight, this card would suggest that you may explore a new path or a new way of doing things. Be open to new ideas that are put to you.

Career

New opportunity or growth. There is an offer to consider.

Love

In established relationships, the return of romance or reconnecting with your partner and if you are single, this is the card we look for to signify someone is coming your way. Remember it is a Cups card falling in its natural environment of emotional upliftment, so love will be amplified in a reading.

Health

If you have a health concern and you have the Knight of Cups appearing, it may suggest that a solution is coming your way, or for you to be open to advice. You could be exploring options as well as looking at metaphysical solutions.

Card Combinations with Knight of Cups

The Lovers and Two of Cups: soulmate on their way, or love and commitment reinforced in your life.

Ace of Wands: a job offer coming towards you

The Devil: depressed young man

Four of Wands: marriage proposal

As an Outcome Card

As this card is a favourable card promising opportunity, love and solutions, it is a Yes card.

QUEEN OF CUPS

Buzz words: Feminine, artistic, spiritual, mother or female relation, water sign

Abstract buzz words: Positive emotions, fantasy, therapy and marriage guidance, success through trusting your intuition and following your plans

General Meaning

The Queen of Cups signifies an extremely feminine woman. She is artistic, often psychic, and is highly imaginative. There may be mediumistic abilities or an inclination towards the spiritual path. Her talents may be underused for at times, she lacks the drive or confidence found in the other Queens. This Queen often appears in spreads as a woman who is related to you (e.g. mother or sister). In love, she is sympathetic and very loving. She may have trouble asserting herself and always puts her man first. She is prone to bursting into tears and is tender hearted towards weaker souls, those in distress and small animals.

As an abstract card, the Queen of Cups can suggest a world of fantasy and fiction. This may be expressed through books and films. She can represent emotional therapy, family therapy and marriage guidance. When negative, this could mean repressed emotions, blocked sexuality, self-pity and being full of drama. Negatively aspected, this card could also be interpreted as a changeable, over emotional woman. She could be an emotional 'vampire' that drains lovers, friends or colleagues. When I say negatively aspected, I refer to the Devil, any negative swords cards, or lots of number Five cards around; irrespective of suit.

Finances

Money may be an emotional area for you, and security is important. Trust your gut instincts around money matters. You may be spending money on running the home, since this queen is considered 'the motherly queen'. Any queen appearing in any sector of life - whether it is in finances or career - may be instrumental in helping. So, if you have an issue and a Queen comes up for finances, it would be suggestive of asking or taking advice from a female around you.

Career

In the career sector, this card could relate to community service or welfare as it is about family and relationships. It may even be that the querent is a stay at home mum. Again, a court card appearing here will mean that a woman will be helpful (as long as the card next to it is positive). With the Queen of Cups being associated with emotions, one maybe seeking fulfillment in what they do or that career balances home life. Money may not be the driver for career decisions, but emotional satisfaction and working in with their home or personal life. Remember that the Cups suit heighten intuition, so it is important to trust your gut instincts with decisions concerning career and the people you deal with in your working life. Emotional maturity may also be required with what is currently happening.

Love

Motherhood, family bonds, holding the family together, being a wife or partner, feeling emotional, wanting to feel loved and cherished. When Cups fall in a love reading or within a love context question, there is definitely a heartfelt connection. Cups and love go hand in hand and are what we look for in love readings.

Health

Women's issues, motherhood, feeling emotional, emotional wellbeing

Card Combinations with Queen of Cups

The Hermit: marriage counselling or counselling for women

Page of Cups: mother and daughter/son relationship

Three of Pentacles: home maker

As an Outcome Card

Yes, and feeling happy or fulfilled about the result

KING OF CUPS

Buzz words: Imaginative, emotional charismatic, father figures, husbands, partners, water sign

Abstract buzz words: Cultural and spiritual activities

General Meaning

The imaginative King of Cups represents the most feminine of the four kings. He is usually highly intuitive, and often found in creative jobs or industries. His hunches may lead him to be very successful. His presence is often powerfully charismatic. Many people find him magnetic, but difficult. He can make a dangerous enemy, rarely forgetting a betrayal or slight and able to wait for revenge. In love, he is highly sexed and emotional. On the one hand he can be kind and thoughtful, on the other he imagines insults where none are intended. He can be moody and prone to jealousy when negatively aspected (if reversed or with Devil card next to it or close by). If reversed or with negative cards beside the King of Cups, it could play out as a heavy drinker or someone who tries to escape emotionally, hence depression is often associated with this card.

This card can stand for new age businesses and movements, alternate or spiritual ideals. Secret organisations, especially those with occult overtones. Also, this King denotes a wide range of artistic and cultural activities.

Finances

A water sign male or someone related giving advice or helping with finances. The cups often represent someone who is related to us appearing in a reading. The cups appearing in the financial sector often represent how we feel about our finance or choices, rather than our actions. We may need to look at whether we are just talking about ideas instead of putting them into action.

Career

A male could be helpful in giving advice or have your back. You may need to focus more on the tasks at hand. There is a passive energy around your working life. You may need to have more drive as this King is not as focused as the other Kings - he is cruisy about work; however, he may still get places as he can read human nature. The King of Cups can describe careers that have spiritual/health or wellbeing overtones or connections to.

Love

This is the husband card if you are looking for 'the one'. You may feel an emotional connection and feel emotionally supported by a special someone in your life. If you are single, a court card in a relationship reading will indicate that you will meet someone. This male will be charismatic, could be prone to being jealous but at least he will make his feelings known. I urge you to look at cards beside the court cards to see whether they are they positive - if you see the Devil around please take notice as this will show a dark side to the person. We want to see bright happy cards in love readings. If you see a run of negative cards and the Moon is hanging around too, please be on guard.

Health

The King of Cups appearing in a health reading will indicate that you may be seeing a health professional or be guided to see someone. This could relate to your emotional health.

Card Combinations with King of Cups

The Devil: drinking or other addictive habit to avoid dealing with emotions, depression
Queen of Cups: husband and wife, mother and father
Any Page: father/child relationship

The Magician and High Priestess: new age leader or figure

As an Outcome Card

Yes, feeling secure about direction or result. The outcome could be influenced by a male.

PAGE OF PENTACLES

Buzz words: Steady good-natured personality, issues with weight problems or a very sweet tooth, earth sign
Abstract buzz words: Small gains

General Meaning

As an abstract card, this Page signifies news about money or minor property matters. There could be small financial improvements such as a minor rise in salary or some interest on investments. There is good news surrounding family, close friends or children. If reversed or if the Devil card is near, money could be tight right now or there could be unexpected bills to pay.

Finances

When the Page appears, you can expect to enjoy small financial gains. You may need to tackle one financial goal at a time. The Page will often turn up as a credit to your account or interest paid on dividends. We may think that we are playing small or we are not reaping big financial rewards right now but remember that consistent action will result in long term success.

Career

In terms of position, you may be reporting to someone or learning the ropes, so to speak as the Page is still at the beginning of his or her career. You may be moving up the ladder, but don't be in a hurry. Take one step at a time. Career may involve teaching or training, especially if the Hermit is next to it.

Love

You may need to demonstrate your love by buying little gifts of appreciation or doing little things. Sometimes in a reading, a Page will show someone who is younger than the client as a prospective love or someone who is youthful in character.

Health

The guidance of this card is to tackle one thing at a time. Sugar or a love of sweets could be an issue. Need to tackle any health concerns practically.

Card Combinations with Page of Pentacles

Eight of Pentacles: book keeping course or a course that is very practical

Nine of Cups: watch out for weight gain creeping up on you

The Hermit: teacher/student, training and assessment

As an Outcome Card

Positive on a small scale, but still a win.

KNIGHT OF PENTACLES

Buzz words: Ambition and determination, earth sign male, business offer, steady income
Abstract buzz words: Taking steps towards security

General Meaning

This Knight may be just starting out in life, yet his determined brand of ambition will eventually propel him to the top. He is hardworking, patient and rather conventional. At times he may seem slow and a little dull, for his earthly mind may lack imagination. However, is he honest and forthright and makes a loyal friend or partner who will not throw in the towel at the first hurdle.

This card shows the ability to work hard and tenaciously towards a goal. Money may not be abundant, however with a firm aim in sight, future rewards are more than likely. This card also stands for savings, investment etc. Negatively aspected issues with finances are feeling overextended or trying to keep up with debts.

Finances

Steady growth around finances, working diligently to achieve financial success. When a Pentacles card falls in relation to a finance question, it would mean more money coming or being able to negotiate monetary terms. Or, if you are asking about a person, they have a good work ethic and good earning capabilities.

Career

Business offer or proposition. Moving up the corporate ladder or moving up the ranks. Striving steadily ahead. If the Hierophant is close by, could work in financial institution, banking or accounting. If you had a question about a job, it would be the 'steady' option.

Love

The pentacles are very reliable, steady and down to earth but sometimes they forget about romance. If you are married, this card could be suggestive of marriage or a relationship being rock solid or steady and stable. If single, it could be describing an earth sign male who is yet to make an appearance. When we have court cards, they generally relate to people so even if you are married, someone could be trying to chat you up. You don't know what is around the corner, so keep an open mind.

Health

Pentacles are all about routines, so do you need to have routine tests or incorporate a routine to optimize your health? Nutrition is important for earth signs, so you may need to watch what you are eating.

Card Combinations with Knight of Pentacles

Ace of Pentacles: negotiating for a loan or new venture
The Hierophant: discussions with bank, financial planner or broker
Seven of Pentacles: investing in your own business

As an Outcome Card

This is a Yes card, with steady growth or an offer

QUEEN OF PENTACLES

Buzz words: Supportive, practical, kind, earth sign woman
Abstract buzz words: Rewards and treats

General Meaning

This queen represents a warm-hearted woman who is fond of luxury, food, good clothes and elegant places. She often has an instinct for history and is drawn to antiques and old buildings. As a friend, she can provide practical support in a crisis. She is kind and loving but does need a financially stable partner. She dislikes noisy surroundings, failure and has a strong aversion to poverty. In business she is often successful and has a good understanding of management, budgeting and organization. She works hard and will tolerate boring activities if they are likely to lead to something better.

As an abstract card, this Queen could appear when you are in the period of very hard work and suggests rewarding yourself with indulgent treats, e.g. a holiday, jewellery etc. Negatively aspected, she may have a very selfish attitude towards money.

Finances

If your question was something like, "will my finances improve?" the appearance of this Queen will mean that through hard work, playing it safe or being conservative, you will accomplish your financial goals. As a person this Queen is hard working, loyal and reliable as an employee - she would make an excellent employee, therefore a good financial investment. There may be a focus on managing money and getting organized financially to achieve financial goals such as buying nice furnishings or luxury items.

Career

It is likely you are entering a period of hard work where your talents in managing others will not go unnoticed. This Queen may represent a person in your working life that helps you (if cards beside her are positive) or gives you grief if negative cards beside her. And alone, this card denotes business accomplishment and success. This Queen is resilient, strong and will keep going as she is in for the long haul. She is not a quitter.

Love

As an abstract word she stands for loyalty and reliability within a relationship. As a person this Queen likes men who are reliable and that she can depend on even though in reality, she doesn't need them to survive. If you are single, you could be meeting an earth sign female, or she could be instrumental in introducing you to someone new.

Health

This Queen being an earth sign and a natural worrier, will Google all health matters. Stop Googling. Instead, take a practical approach. Go and see a doctor or health care professional and put your mind at rest. Earth signs can be the hypochondriacs of the zodiac, so it is important they address their worry and be proactive to minimize weeks of unnecessary torture.

Card Combinations with Queen of Pentacles

Three of Pentacles: antique dealer or restoring furniture

Queen of Pentacles and Eight of Pentacles: book keeper

The Hermit: a Virgo woman (as opposed to any other earth sign as the Hermit is ruled by Virgo)

The Empress: a woman who loves luxury or brands…hit me with some Prada!

As an Outcome Card

Yes, a positive outcome due to making informed choices, working hard or taking a conservative approach.

KING OF PENTACLES

Buzz words: Financial security, Earth sign male, making solid financial decisions, moving steadily forward, financial caution, being conservative

Abstract buzz words: Gradual material improvement

General Meaning

This King represents a responsible, cautious individual. This man has an excellent head for business although he is certainly not an entrepreneur or speculator. His patience pays off instead. Since material possessions are important to him, he usually has something tucked away for a rainy day and is often well off. In relationships, he is reliable and loyal once he has made up his mind about you, but it is indeed a slow process. He likes the good things in life and prefers the traditional and things that are well made and have stood the test of time. He can be possessive, but the overriding need is for a sense of security. He may not be stimulating like the other Kings, but he is soothing and steadfast. Negatively aspected, he can be a miser and a stick in the mud. When signifying an abstract meaning, the King of Pentacles augurs financial improvement, promotion and the gradual establishment of a profession or business. Banking and finance come under this card

Finances

When the King of Pentacles appears within a finance reading or a finance position within a reading, there is a focus on investments for the future and this could include talking to banks or financial institutions, especially if the Hierophant is close. The Hierophant represents a large institution and with the Pentacles beside it, would mean a bank as opposed to another type of industry.

Career

You are at the top of your game for now - you have worked really hard and will reap the rewards. You may need to play it safe or take the conservative option if you have a career question. This is a solid card for career prospects and money could be driving your decision making.

Love

This is your tall, dark and handsome in a reading – well, he *was*, if you're married ha-ha. With love questions, you need to take the buzzwords and apply them, so if you are asking about a romantic interest, and he is dependable, honest, reliable and good with money, make sure the Devil isn't close by as that could easily turn into 'tight with money'. If single, a mature earth sign male or someone who has dark features maybe showing up in your life.

Health

The King of Pentacles within the context of a health reading would indicate that you will be able to handle any concerns better than you think. A male could be helping or giving you advice regarding health or wellbeing. Taking a conservative approach will see long term success.

Card Combinations with King of Pentacles

Four of Pentacles: obsessed with materialism and money for the future
The Hierophant-: a bank manager or financial analyst
The Hermit: A Virgo male (as opposed to any other Earth sign as the Hermit is ruled by Virgo)

As an Outcome Card

This is a solid card with a positive outcome. It heralds success around finances in particular.

PAGE OF SWORDS

Buzz words: The awakening mind, intellect, communication, gossip, chatty

Abstract buzz words: Communication signifies news, contracts, documents and new plans.

General Meaning

The Page of Swords denotes a well-coordinated, bright young person who enjoys playing games and sports. This Page is very communicative and loves talking and socialising, hence they would have a lot of friends.

This Page suggests enjoying gossip and scandal if reversed or negatively aspected. If reversed or coupled with negative cards beside this Page, it could indicate spiteful gossip, bullying, hurtful texts, messages, lies white and grey. Cyber bullying.

Finances

News or communication around money matters, bank statements or property matters. Contracts that have a financial implication are also governed by this card. You could be discussing, researching or Googling information regarding financial queries. If you have been waiting for news regarding a loan or a property offer, expect to hear some news.

Career

The Page of Swords is a communication card, so it does govern industries or roles with communication and media. If the World, Moon and Six of Wands fall in a career reading, the client may be a public or well-known figure. This Page also dictates learning, so courses or workshops may be coming up for the client. If the client is undecided about studying, it would be suggestive of being beneficial for career advancement or may look good on their resume.

Love

The Page of Swords can indicate a text, phone call, or email from a potential love interest if single. It may also mean online dating as this card also governs technology and communication. If married or in a relationship, there could be a need to communicate more. In itself it is a positive card, however if you have the pesky Seven of Swords next to it, don't trust the information that you are receiving; someone maybe feeding you half-truths or lies.

Health

This would pertain to news about your health or Googling health matters. With the Swords, they are also medical cards as knives remind us of needles or surgical instruments. Minor health issues could be coming up such as dentist, doctors or blood test.

Card Combinations with Page of Swords

Queen of Swords: a very sharp woman who doesn't miss a thing! If you also had the Devil or another negative card, it would conjure up the word 'bitchy'.

Three of Swords and The Moon: blood test

Any other Page: group of students or children

The Magician and The World: linguist

Seven of Cups: communication via phone

The Moon, Seven of Swords, Five of Cups and The Lovers: online porn or adult sites

As an Outcome Card

The Page of Swords is a news card and depending on whether the cards around it are positive, then the news should be too. In any case, there is an update on matters or you hear news about something you have been waiting on

KNIGHT OF SWORDS

Buzz words: Quick thinking, needing to slow down, new ideas
Abstract buzz words: Speed and change

General Meaning

The Knight of Swords represents a confident, articulate young man with blossoming reasoning powers and subtle wit. Physically restless, he acts quickly, and sometimes impetuously. This card may represent people who work in public relations or the media. As an abstract card, the Knight of Swords rushes into a spread like a powerful gust of wind. This symbolises that fresh air may sweep through your life, bringing sudden change, new ideas and fresh plans. There is a feeling of surprise which pervades information you receive at this time; whether letters, phone calls or encounters. An old friend may suddenly reappear in your life. Look to surrounding cards as to which area is most affected by this unexpected surge of energy. Negatively aspected, this card means deceit, someone being sly or misleading.

Finances

The Knight of Swords can be impetuous, so it does warn about not rushing into making financial decisions without carefully looking at the fine print. If you need to make a swift decision which this Knight may signify, make sure that the cards beside it are good, solid Pentacle cards, not the Devil or the Ten of Wands, as your swift decision could be costly or cause you to carry a financial burden (Ten of Wands).

Career

When the Knight of Swords appears in the career sector, you can expect some sweeping changes, or a new manager may implement new ideas or processes. You may need to think on your feet and make quick decisions. It could describe a very hectic work environment. If you were making a decision about career, it would be prudent to think about things before making a rash decision, however you may have a deadline for your response.

Love

There is a harshness to this card within a love reading. It often signifies someone who has no filter and could easily upset another. It could signify a lover coming in very quickly as there is a lot of haste attached to this card. It will
often represent a person in your life and there is a sense of trying to win you over, as this Knight is very competitive. At least when this card appears, life is not boring, that is for sure.

Health

You are rushing -slow down. Do not jump to conclusions where your health is concerned. More care is needed.

Card Combinations with Knight of Swords

Justice: speeding or parking fine

The Chariot: motor bike

The Devil and Five of Swords: rage, arguments erupting, cautioning you to watch your personal safety

The Chariot and King of Swords: highway patrol

As an Outcome Card

You need to remember this is a Knight, and they are always chivalrous, so it is likely that the outcome is what you are hoping for or someone comes to the rescue with a solution.

QUEEN OF SWORDS

Buzz words: Cool, charming, intelligent, air sign female, single, ex-partner, mistress, widow

Abstract buzz words: Success in mental pursuits e.g. public speaking, detachment, discerning writing, music, the arts

General Meaning

This Queen represents an intelligent, perceptive woman. Like her masculine counterpart, she is rational and logical. In all but the extreme situations, her heart is firmly ruled by her, quick witted head. She loves a lively social life, needing the stimulation of other people's ideas and enjoying wide ranging conversation. Her friendships are rarely deep for she prefers to skim the surface and likes variety. She can be strong and clear headed in a crisis. In love, this Queen shies away from possessive or over emotional types. She is firm believer in sexual equality and likes to talk about problems. She is graceful and likes to look nice. This Queen is often the unavailable woman in a spread who is having an affair or is single in status. Negatively aspected, this woman is 'bitchy', bitter and a gossip. If reversed, this Queen is a trouble maker who is spreading rumors about you or who is jealous or does things in spite. She can be dangerous as she is clever.

Finances

Needing to be smart with money and take the emotion out of decision making regarding any financial decision. A woman may be giving you sound financial advice or assistance. Investing in your education maybe a good investment for the future.

Career

The appearance of this Queen in a career reading suggests you act professionally and keep your emotions in check. You need to think with your head and not your heart. You need to be politically correct and play your cards right. This Queen is smart and has an agenda. She has a game plan, and no one will get in her way. If this represents a person in your reading, she could be a formidable opponent. If it represents you being like this Queen, it will be helpful to whatever is playing out. Being smart is the operative word. It governs the intellect, so could relate to a job where you may need to think rationally and be articulate. Court cards are nearly always people; they either help or hinder you, so look at the surrounding cards to ascertain what energy is surrounding the court cards or upcoming events.

Love

In a love reading for a female if this represents you, you may love your independence as this Queens screams personal freedom compared to the other queens. You may be feeling icy towards your partner or may need more mental stimulation. This Queen loves to be challenged. As a person, she represents an air sign female. Often in a complicated love reading this will represent the meddling or troublesome ex-wife or partner.

Health

The Queen of Swords asks you to be mindful of your body and pay attention to the signals it is giving you. Do not be afraid to ask for help or seek the appropriate advice at this time.

Card Combinations with Queen of Swords

Seven of Swords: 'frenemy'
Death: a widow (this is to describe the person, not an upcoming event)
The Lovers and Strength: someone who works in beauty/makeup/wellbeing and related fields.
The Devil: bitch

As an Outcome Card

To obtain a positive outcome, you need to be smart about the matter at hand and because you will be smart, you will succeed.

KING OF SWORDS

Buzz words: Logical, clever and quick witted
Abstract buzz words: Advice, intellect

General Meaning

The King of Swords represents a clever, well-educated man with a particular gift for logical argument and rational thought. He often stands for a lawyer, doctor or psychologist. Nine times out of ten, you will find him working in some professional capacity where his bright and restless mind can be put to good use. In matters of love, this King can be a little chilly and lacking in substance. He feels emotion but has difficulty in expressing it with his key phrase being, "I think", rather than "I feel". He is a charming flirt and requires a lot of mental stimulation from friends and lovers.

As an abstract card, this King stands for good, clear advice. This can be about work or refer to legal matters, depending on surrounding cards. Negatively aspected or reversed, this King can be manipulative and play devil's advocate in arguments or play mind games. If in business and this card is negatively aspected, watch out for contracts full of traps for the unwary. This King can be a silver-tongued liar.

Finances

Professional advice being sought or offered regarding financial or property matters. The King of Swords often denotes a solicitor, especially if the Justice card is hanging around. If the Four of Wands is close by, it could be a real estate agent giving you advice, or you may decide to go with a particular agent, put your property on the market or purchase a property. This King often refers to advice from a professional, so it is advisable to explore your options or do your research before making a decision.

Career

This King could represent an authority figure that assists you in achieving your goals or mentors you. He may be very intellectual or have a degree as this King is often well qualified. If the Justice Card appears next to this King, it can represent industries such as the legal field or law enforcement. If the Magician was next to this King, the client could be a specialist or be in a niche field. This King suggests you be politically correct and think with your head and not your emotions if you want to achieve success or climb the ladder. This King has a well-executed plan and probably a sales funnel.

Love

The King of Swords represents an air sign male in a reading that could be turning up. If you are married, you may be needing to discuss matters rationally or you may need to communicate more. The keywords or abstract meaning can be applied, which is seeking advice or communication.

Health

The King of Swords in a health-related question will indicate a doctor or seeing someone professional about your current concern. Do not hesitate to seek advice at this time.

Card Combinations with King of Swords

Justice: upholder of law, e.g. policeman or lawyer
Justice and the Emperor: a judge
Three of Swords and Page of Swords: a doctor
Strength: alternate therapists, such as chiropractor or naturopath
Eight of Wands/The World/The Chariot: pilot
The Chariot/Two of Pentacles: sailor or master mariner

The Hermit: psychologist

The Hermit and The Magician: psychiatrist (remember that the Magician is always a master or a specialist in something)

As an Outcome Card

Follow advice from a professional person.

PAGE OF WANDS

Buzz words: Feeling more creative, message, a book, news, reading, expressing your creativity through words

Abstract buzz words: Short journeys, invitations and plenty of lively conversation.

General Meaning

The Page of Wand represents a lively, intelligent child or teenager of either sex. More frequently, it represents the upsurge of energy and dawning of creativity. It brings positive influence similar to the Knight, but to a lesser extent. When negative, this Page denotes delayed communications and slow progress in business and property matters. Cancellation of event.

Finances

Doing research or reading up on material about financial matters. Taking small steps to achieve financial goals. A Page can represent a younger person, so you may be assisting a younger person financially, or the matter could relate to a child financially. Connect a buzzword to the area of life you are enquiring about to give you the energy and outcome of the question. In relation to finances, it suggests scoping out ideas as it could lead to making some good decisions. The wands are about applying some action to your thoughts, so you will have to follow through with the idea to see the benefit.

Career

The appearance of the Page of Wands may see you wanting to express yourself creatively. This Page brings new life to projects, inspiration or new ideas. You may want to do some research or get more involved in what you are doing to obtain a better understanding. If the Hermit is next to it, it often represents teaching or learning, so can signify a student or a teacher. If it has the High Priestess next to it, the person will often be a psychic reader or someone learning a spiritual or psychic modality. The Page may also be suggestive of someone still learning the ropes, as the Page is often young or inexperienced in some respects.

Love

If you have been waiting on a potential love interest to text or phone you, the Page is a messenger card. Messaging or the way you communicate may be a focus. The Page could represent a fire sign person - male or female - that is yet to appear. As a love card, it is about the way one expresses their emotions and with this Page, they would express themselves with actions. Actions speak louder than words.

Health

As a messenger card, you may be hearing news about health or you could be taking action in optimizing your health. Researching ways to improve health could be amplified. It is an action card, so implementing some exercise could be helpful also.

Card Combinations with Page of Wands

The High Priestess: psychic reading, spiritual books and learning

The Hermit: study, teacher/student

Queen of Cups: mother/child relationship

As an Outcome Card

You will receive news about the matter soon. Scope out ideas, for it will lead to bigger things.

KNIGHT OF WANDS

Buzz words: Drive, new energy, new job, new home, offers
Abstract buzz words: Movement, activity, visitors, short trips, job offer, house move

General Meaning

The impetuous Knight of Wands represents a gregarious, intelligent young man. This character has great plans for the future and with his energy and creativity, he will eventually succeed. However, at this stage of life he has little staying power, is easily bored by the daily grind, and better at starting projects than following them through. Sometimes this can indicate an older man who has a boyish character and attitude to life. Negatively aspected, this man is a charming rogue, hard to resist but not to be trusted.

Finances

Movement around finances. This could also relate to a potential house move or spending money on travelling. If finances have been tight, expect new energy to flow in through either a new job or a change you make. You may need to take some action around your finances if you want to achieve growth. Remember it is an action card, so you must apply an action to get a different result. It is a positive omen around financial matters as it signifies movement to the status quo.

Career

This is the card we are looking for when we are looking for a job change. This represents job offers or new opportunities. It brings in new energy and a desire for change. If the

Emperor or the King of Wands is next to it, the profession could be the army or defense force. If the Four of Wands is next to it, real estate. In any case, it is a positive card in relation to career and denotes positive change.

Love

For singles, a Knight appearing means someone on the horizon. This King represents a fire sign male. If the Emperor is close by, he could be ex-army or reserves, so you can glean some more information about this person. If you are in a relationship, you could be travelling or there will be more interaction in your life. This Knight brings more excitement as you may be exploring new places to visit or meeting new people.

Health

Exercise and getting out and about is what you need to feel better about yourself. Accept invitations or try new activities.

Card Combinations with Knight of Wands

Four of Wands: real estate matters

Ten of Pentacles or The World: house move, travel

The Emperor: armed forces, ex-army, defence force, works for government.

As an Outcome Card

A positive card. It is a Yes card as it carries a lot of energy.

QUEEN OF WANDS

Buzz words: Warm, light and loyal, opinionated, assertive woman
Abstract buzz words: success, self-confidence, inner strength, rural, countryside

General Meaning

The Queen of Wands is an independent, charismatic woman. She makes a great friend, since she is generous and hospitable. She is full of bright ideas and can be helpful to those she loves. She loves to have fun and enjoys lively company. In love, she is passionate and sensual. She brings a sense of humor to her relationships and can have a fiery temper. Reversed or negatively aspected, negative traits of the fire sign could arise, such as bossiness and arrogance.

Finances

Needing to take control of finances or be assertive about financial affairs. Going after what you want financially. This Queen is fiery and knows what she wants and is prepared to fight for what is hers. Be prepared to listen however, and do not let your pride get in the way of making a sound financial decision.

Career

Enterprising business woman with a strong sense of self. This Queen can be very confident and makes a great friend, but a fiery competitor. The energy of this Queen suggests you back your ideas, keep motivated and driven to succeed. This Queen could be helpful to you in your career if you schmooze and don't get on her bad side. She loves to be praised.

Love

This Queen is a fire sign and is fiercely loyal but could have a quick temper if pushed. As an abstract meaning, it would suggest loyalty and generosity within a relationship. It would also encourage being independent and assertive.

Health

This Queen being from the Wands suit again, suggests that any physical activity (walking, Zumba, dancing, sport) would be beneficial for keeping fit and looking after your health. You can also look at ailments associated with fire signs.

Card Combinations with Queen of Wands

The Magician: a female business leader
The Devil: a female narcissist, victim

As an Outcome Card

Positive outcomes are associated with this card due to it being a Queen which is a sign of maturity. It is also an action card.

KING OF WANDS

Buzz words: Drive, integrity, entrepreneur, fire sign
Abstract buzz words: Negotiations and agreements, wheeling and dealing

General Meaning

The King of Wands often represents an energetic, vital man you are likely to encounter at work or through business connections. He is a strong character, with a good sense of humor and is usually good company. He is fair minded and is full of ideas with the drive to back them up. He often finds considerable success. In his private life, he is fun loving and probably the larrikin of all the Kings. He likes the countryside, fresh air, and sport. Reversed or negatively aspected, he may be selfish and freedom loving.

Finances

Receiving advice from an entrepreneur type character. Taking control of your finances or exploring options for future wealth or investments.

Career

This could represent an authority figure at your workplace or could represent you. This is the card for someone who shows entrepreneurial skills and is a born leader, and it denotes great business success and acumen. If the Emperor is close by, it could be the defense force as describing someone's occupation or potential occupation. You can learn a lot about someone in your career that has this King's energy as they can predict long term trends or have long term visions that some people are not able to see. He is usually a fair person with a good sense of humor. In itself, it you were worried about your career, this card suggests success.

Love

This King represents a fire sign male, usually a happy go lucky type of character that may sweep you off your feet. A court card within a reading most of the time represents a person that interacts with you. If you cannot place this person it could be someone you meet, but if it relates to a question about your existing relationship, it could mean that the other person may hold a lot of power or be influencing you. It is not a negative card and there is lots of communication with this card, so don't hold back.

Health

A male could be helping you with any health or wellbeing concern. This could be an alternate health provider, especially if the Strength card is next to it. Keeping your mind and body active is important.

Card Combinations with King of Wands

Four of Wands: real estate agent

The Emperor: defense force

Four of Wands and The Magician: auctioneer

As an Outcome Card

Positive outcome - this is a Yes card. Lots of energy and drive to succeed with this card

MINOR ARCANA

Minor Arcana Overview

The Minor Arcana consists of the four suits of Wands, Pentacles, Swords and Cups numbered Ace (1) - 10. There is a close association with numerology, so I am going to list the basic meanings below, so you learn a quick way to understand the numbering. You can also look at the imagery and the colour of the cards to ignite your intuition.

NUMBER ASSOCIATION

One (Ace)

Key Word: *Beginnings*

New beginnings, opportunity, potential, drive, ideas, inspiration and aspiration. One deals with that which is about to take form. Seeing multiple Aces indicates that a situation is about to begin or is in the early stages of development. Master number 11 is a high vibration number, so ensure that you keep your thoughts positive as this is a manifestation number.

Two

Key Word: *Relationships and Partnerships*

Partnerships and relationships, balance, duality, a crossroad or choice, agreement and insight. Needing to see others point of view.

Three

Key Word: *Growth and Collaboration*

Initial achievement of goals, growth, creativity, abundance, expression, communication and friendships. The number 3 is the cementing factor of 1 and 2 and goes through to 4 to bring about that which is desired and envisioned. Multiple 3s can indicate group activities or situations involving more than one person.

Four

Key Word: *Foundations and Structures*

Structure, foundation, stability, stagnation, manifestation, practical application, formation, concentration, organisation and planning. It is the result of a well-built foundation and proper application. It is what comes as a result of desire and imagination (i.e. the energy of 1, 2 and 3). Many 4s can indicate fruition or the manifestation of an idea along with a foundation where things can grow.

Five

Key Word: *Change and the Need to Adapt*

Instability, conflict, loss, opportunity for change, new cycle, change, expansion and recreation. Multiple 5s indicate change, challenge and fluctuation. They also indicate material prosperity, but spiritual poverty if not properly balanced.

Six

Keywords: *Home Life, Love, and Moving forward from Problems*

Communication, problem-solving, cooperation, balance, relaxation, adjustment, harmony, compassion, social consciousness, domesticity, love, care, comfort and concern. Many 6s indicates adjustments in thoughts, attitudes or conditions. They also represent the ability to transcend difficulties.

Seven

Keywords: *Reflection and Wisdom*

Reflection, assessment, motives, spirituality, wisdom, perfect order, observation, investigation, meditation, discovery and knowledge. Seven represents faith – faith in the things that can't be seen, but nevertheless exist. It is about knowing the ultimate truth, and it is through experience that understanding develops and faith in the unknown is attained. Many 7s indicate a period of introspection or solitude. 777 can also indicate repetitive patterns where you need to break the cycle.

Eight

Keyword: Success and Money

Movement, action, change, rebirth, regeneration, re-evaluation, capability, spiritual fortitude, success, recognition, accomplishment and attainment. Eight is associated with power that springs from within and enables one to accomplish that which one sets out to do. Many 8s indicate a positive change of mind or status.

Nine

Keywords: Fulfilment Attainment of Goals

Fruition, attainment, bringing things to a conclusion, completion, fulfilment, selflessness, magnetism, idealism and giver of wisdom or inspiration. Repetitive 9s mean that situations or events are nearing completion or have just been completed and another plateau awaits.

Ten

Keywords: Ends and Beginnings

Completion, end of a cycle and renewal. 10 can also become 1 (1+0 = 1) and therefore the tens represent the same things as the Aces, but on a higher level. Repetitive 10s can indicate endings which will soon transform into new beginnings

SUMMARY ON TAROT SUITS

PENTACLES	WANDS	CUPS	SWORDS
Wealth Health Physical	Creativity Action Passion	Love Emotion Empathy	Thought Challenge Observation
Winter	Summer	Autumn	Spring
Years	Days	Months	Weeks
Capricorn Taurus Virgo	Aries Leo Sagittarius	Pisces Cancer Scorpio	Aquarius Gemini Libra
Earth	Fire	Water	Air

ACE OF WANDS

Buzz words: New job, new beginnings, taking inspired action, creativity, resurgence of energy, birth, giving birth to

General Meaning

Whether it be a physical birth or the beginning of something new, the Ace of Wands heralds a new beginning in your life. This could pertain to a new job, change of residence or a love interest. Take notice where the Ace is placed within the spread or if you have a single card question - it is suggestive of something new beginning.

Finances

A new beginning around career could see your finances improving. An idea or surge of creativity could be beneficial financially, so follow it through. You could be outlaying funds for something new in your life. If you had the Chariot next to it, you would be purchasing a new car or something on wheels. If it were a motorbike, I would see the Ace of Wands/Chariot/Knight of Swords (speed).

Career

New job. New opportunity being presented. It represents growth and taking inspired action to implement change.

Love

If you are already in a relationship, you may decide to start something together that allows you to grow together. If single, you are entering a new phase. In any case, whether single or in a relationship, you can expect some fresh energy to enter your love life.

Health

This is an action card, so what do you need to do to improve your health? For those wanting to develop medical intuitive words, this card can signify polyps or fibroids, especially if the Empress is close by, however we are not doctors, and we should never diagnose. You have a duty of care not to scare people. Let the professionals do their job. You may want to stay clear of health readings if you do not know how to handle this area delicately. I generally will just include things that are helpful, not detrimental, as you will cause untold grief.

As an Outcome Card

This is an energy card, so it is a Yes card for positive outcomes.

TWO OF WANDS

Buzz words: Planning, plans move forward, enterprising, someone helping you, overcoming difficulties, solutions provided, assistance coming

General Meaning

The Two of Wands is about having thoughts about future direction and goals, and now making decisions to get the ball rolling. You might be exploring new avenues or wanting to maximize your potential. Whatever it may be, as an action card, things start to take shape. As a number 2 card or duality, you may have some anxiety with making these decisions to go outside of your comfort zone. There is a message about feeding your creativity or investing in your personal growth.

Finances

Plans come together, or someone is instrumental in giving you advice or help regarding your finances. As it is a card of balance, you may be balancing your accounts.

Career

Plans to expand your potential are amplified. Helpful people in the career sector that are instrumental in opening doors for you. Scoping out your career path and making plans on how to get ahead. Remember it is an action card, so it is important to not only have a journey plan, a budget or a business plan, but to start to track your progress.

Love

You may need to make more plans with a loved one or if single, focus on plans to have fun and connect with others. If things have been difficult in a relationship or friendship area, there is more balance or harmony coming in.

Health

Since this card is about planning, you could be focusing on preventative health measures as well as taking a balanced approach about any health concerns.

As an Outcome Card

It's a positive card and it recommends that you will see success if you plan and take a balanced approach. Hold the vision as you will succeed

THREE OF WANDS

Buzz words: Goal setting, opportunities, implementing long term strategies, looking at things clearly, successful outcomes, initiative and foresight, plans moving forward, creativity, enterprising, business dealings

General Meaning

Opportunities, planning. When this card appears, opportunities are presenting themselves or you are creating your own opportunities. It is a time of expansion and planning ahead and looking at things from a long-term view point.

Finances

The advice of this card is to budget and write down your goals, and to be accountable with your funds. Explore new opportunities to make money or reduce costs. It's all about maximizing what you can for financial advantage.

Career

When this card appears for a career reading, a new opportunity presents itself. There is a feeling of expansion, getting ahead, and feeling excited about the direction of your future. The answer might be to look at greener pastures or take a long-term approach to things.

Love

Since this card is not one of the traditional love cards, it may describe a characteristic of a person or what their focus is, or it can indeed indicate someone self-confident and optimistic. In a marriage or relationship, it could indicate a partner who is focusing on getting ahead which on the flip side could mean a little less time or focus on their partner. If single, one may be exploring their options.

Health

This means getting a health plan of course or planning for better health. It could also mean looking at different options to tackle health concerns - don't limit yourself.

As an Outcome Card

It is a positive card, heralding expansion in business or in moving forward.

FOUR OF WANDS

Buzz words: Home, real estate, celebration, stability, happiness, solid foundations

General Meaning

When the Four of Wands appears, you can expect things to start settling down or you may have more certainty about future stability and direction. This card rules home and family matters and signifies stability since it's numerical value is 4. So, if you had any concerns with homes and real estate, what you are hoping for will come about soon. If you are wanting more stability or security, then this card suggests that this will come about.

Finances

Saving for a home or investing in property is amplified. Money matters improve or level out.

Career

Real estate or property development/styling could be a career path, or there could be an association with the building industry. Since this is a card of celebrations, it could also indicate event planning, especially if you had the Three of Pentacles or Eight of Pentacles next to it. In any case, take the essence of the card which is 'stability' and know that the career area becomes stable, or if you are looking for work, there is something more stable being offered.

Love

The Four of Wands always means a happy union with commitment. We often see this come up for engagements, weddings or when celebrating milestones. It is one of the love cards we like to see in a reading, as it reassures us there is a good foundation to build on.

Health

The key phrase that would apply to health is 'sticking to routines'. Since the number 4 is about stability, it would suggest taking a proactive approach, incorporating daily practices to be beneficial for your wellbeing. Remember it is a positive card, so use the advice of the card to optimize your health as well as seeking the advice of a medical practitioner.

As an Outcome Card

It's a positive, uplifting, happy card, so it is a Yes card.

FIVE OF WANDS

Buzz words: Arguments, competition, strife, disagreements, challenge, under attack, need to change what you are doing

General Meaning

When the Five of Wands appears, be warned about potential conflict. Depending on your question, be prepared to have either conflicting views, competition or some angst. The advice is: be keep calm and be respectful to others' viewpoints. At this point in time, you are not on the same page. You may feel challenged as this is the card of strife and tension. Know that this too, shall pass.

Finances

Conflict over money, feeling angst over the state of your financial affairs, could be more money going out than coming in. Spending money on unnecessary items.

Career

Look out for competition. The environment in the work place could be testing you, but the message is to persevere and rise and above it - don't let people get to you - push back. The environment at work is competitive, so you must have confidence in yourself and your abilities, so you are not walked over.

Love

This card turning up in a relationship reading can often be predictive and foretells arguments. One party could feel defensive or may feel under attack. If you are single, you might feel there is no one out there for you or that it is hard dating. This card warns to you not to feel persecuted by others but instead, to work on your self-confidence.

Health

Stress is showing up in the health area. Feeling niggly. Needing to unwind and let go of things you cannot control.

As an Outcome Card

This is a challenging card, so the outcome would be in line with the nature of the card. If you follow this path it could be difficult, or you may need to be prepared to be challenged. I would draw another clarifying card. If it is negative, it will amplify the difficulty, or if positive, it will show that the angst can be overcome. In itself, it is a No card.

SIX OF WANDS

Buzz words: victory, accolades, affluency, prestige, feeling good, positive negotiations, success around work, good outcomes around money matters, feeling good enough, raising your standards /pricing/ value, being in the spotlight / time to shine, achievements

General Meaning

This is the card of accolades, prestige, or feeling affluent as a result of getting ahead, being acknowledged, receiving praise or a promotion. If you are waiting on news or a development, the feedback is positive or will have successful outcomes. Your self-esteem rises as a result of validation; however, one must remember that true validation comes from within. When this card appears, we can expect things to run smoothly or even better than we expect.

Finances

Good news, developments. Your worth is determined by money. There is an association between what you think of yourself and a corresponding vibrational match in terms of finances. Successful financial negotiations or offers.

Career

Praise, accomplishment and negotiation skills. It's a great card to draw if you have a work-related question as it always denotes success. Should the Six of Wands appear for a work question, your self-importance or sense of self will increase accordingly. How you present yourself is also amplified - you may have to conform to a certain standard, image or culture.

Love

Self-esteem, self-love is highlighted as a key to attracting more love into your life. Everyone loves you when you love yourself and think highly of yourself (not in an up yourself sort of way). You may be raising your standards in the love area.

Health

Focusing on self-esteem is the key.

As an Outcome Card

The Six of Wands is a Yes card as the key words are successful outcomes.

SEVEN OF WANDS

Buzz words: defend your position, feeling pissed off, overwhelmed, too much to do, under attack, feeling down, people being nasty, don't give up, stand up for your beliefs, lessons learnt

General Meaning

The Seven of Wands turns up when we are overwhelmed. In this headspace, we are defending our beliefs, values, principles or boundaries. You may need to think before you speak, or why you even find yourself in this position. Boundary issues with others raises its head for you to enforce your personal space while you sort out the matters you need to attend to. There is nothing wrong with saying "no" - just be respectful - you do not have to explain yourself. This energy is quite niggly so use any de-stressing techniques or grounding exercises to calm the f$ck down. The Seven of Wands warns not to take on too much, as you can only handle so much before you get yourself into a state.

Finances

This card warns you to not take on any more debt at this time or spend unnecessarily, as you will feel overwhelmed with bills to pay. If you need to make a financial decision, weigh up your present commitment levels and be realistic.

Career

You may have too much to do or aren't delegating enough. You could find yourself defending decisions or your work. As long as you have all your facts correct, defend your position or assert your boundaries respectfully. Consider how you find yourself in this position and if you have allowed it. There is a sense of feeling defeated with this card or that it's all too much. Take a break; don't give up. The message is: prepare for challenge but know that you can move through it.

Love

The Seven of Wands in the love area talks about a clash of wills or not being on the same page. A partner could expect too much of the other and so one feels overwhelmed. On the other hand, a partner could feel under attack for the things that they do. If single, you may not feel good enough or the dating game could be tiring. You need to strengthen your boundaries with people you meet, so you are not wasting your time.

Health

Feeling under the weather, health goals feeling unachievable. The message is: take a break, but don't give up. You have too much on your plate to be able to focus. Look at your priorities - what can you let go of to free up time to include exercise, meditation, yoga or meal prep?

As an Outcome Card

This is a challenging card, so you need to change things to get a different result.

EIGHT OF WANDS

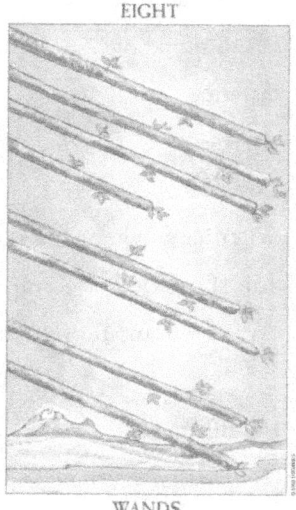

Buzz words: travel, movement, activity, correspondence, yes, busy, productive, success, developments, breakthroughs, ideas, action, power, drive, organization, driving

General Meaning

Things speed up, pick up, and plans move forward. This card can indicate movement, travel. The Eight of Wands appears to let us know that things may develop quickly, the pace picks up, or what we are hoping for will be successful. The numeric value is 8 and is always associated with drive, organization, power and success. If you are wondering about whether something was positive or the outcome beneficial, the answer is yes. Use this energy to get things done or use your organizational talent to keep up with the flourish of activity. It's a Green Light Day. Get Going!

Finances

Money flows in. Loans are approved, or money lent. Decisions of a financial nature gain momentum. If your money sector has been a worry or things have been tight, the Eight of Wands brings activity, enquiry and developments. If business conversion has been slow, it will improve. If it is busy, it will continue to thrive under the influence of the Eight of Wands.

Career

You are on a roll. If you are looking for a job, the prospects are positive and there is a of activity. Work pace picks up and with it comes increased correspondence, action and developments. The Eight of Wands - being a travel card - may also indicate you could be travelling as a result of your employment. If you had the World next to it, you may get to travel overseas, or if the Six of Swords is beside it, you may travel interstate or a distance.

Love

Whether single or married, you could find yourself very popular with invitations to go out. If married or committed, travel plans or doing stuff together is amplified. If single, expect a flourish of invitations or interest.

Health

Get that arse moving. The key to improving health goals is getting active.

As an Outcome Card

The Eight of Wands is the Action card, so it is a Yes Card.

NINE OF WANDS

Buzz words: don't throw in the towel, feeling negative, one week or month, feeling like you have come along way but yet so far to go, feeling like everyone against you, overcoming obstacles but a little bit to go, take a rest, stand your ground, believe in yourself

General Meaning

You haven't come this far, to only come this far. Instead of throwing in the towel, step up the action. Choose the actions of someone who wants to succeed - don't be a quitter. While we may wonder, "what's the point?" you have to think about all the hard work you have put in and the message here is not to throw it away. Obstacles will be overcome with a change in mindset and a different plan of action. You may think people are against you, but that maybe your inner Negative Nancy coming out to play. Take a chill pill, go for a walk, get re-inspired. You may need to finish or finalize things when the Nine of Wands appears - productivity may improve your mood. Instead of quitting, pause or take a rest. A rest is all you may require in order to gather the strength you need to tackle things again.

Finances

Bills could be overwhelming, or you are feeling that you are working hard but not really living, as all you are doing is paying the bills. There is a warning here about not giving in - whether that be to your own temptations of spending, or to others' financial needs. This card brings with it a feeling of not having enough or not being where you want to be, so in the finance sector, this is saying you need to change your perspective and look at how far you have come. While you may not be where you want to be, a negative attitude is not going to help your cause, so take a break, don't give up and know that perseverance and good financial practices will pay off.

Career

You may need to defend your actions. Believe in yourself and not throw in the towel. In terms of fulfilling goals or achieving particular outcomes, you are not quite there yet, but being a 9 means it is close to the end of a cycle, so change is in sight. A little more effort is needed. This card often comes up when we feel uptight or feel like we are not making progress, but we need to take a reality check to see how far we have come.

Love

Not a great card for love as the energy it brings is one of dissatisfaction or wanting to give up. You might have to look at the part you are playing, as often with the Nine of Wands, we may feel inadequate and could be projecting. On the flip side, consider how much investment or time you have put into a relationship and ask yourself whether it worth is giving up on. If you are single, you may feel like giving up on the dating scene or meeting someone. The message is: don't give up, the miracle is just around the corner.

Health

Paranoid about health. Feeling tired. Guidance is to find solutions instead of focusing on the problems.

As an Outcome Card

It is not a positive card, so would indicate there would be blocks or you are needing to overcome some difficulties to get the result you are wanting at this point in time. However, take the advice from the card and don't give up. You just need to have more patience and draw on your resilience until things line up. Draw a clarifying card, and if still negative, revisit your plan of action or what you are doing. If positive, forge forward.

TEN OF WANDS

Buzz words: Carrying a burden, feeling blocked, heavy work load and responsibilities, sore back, end of rut, cycle

General Meaning

The Ten of Wands appearing in a reading always shows a period of hard work, carrying the load or feeling burdened. Often, we are feeling the weight of the world on our shoulders and for this reason, we may feel blocked or unable to see our path or our next step clearly. It is a card of hard work or effort, so just know that it will pay off even though it may not feel this way at the moment.

Finances

If you have a financial decision to make, make sure you are not putting yourself under further pressure. This card warns of financial burdens or feeling weighed down by debt or financial obligations. It might be helpful to examine your beliefs about abundance and the law of attraction.

Career

This often appears when your boss or organization piles more work and responsibility on your shoulders. The feeling of burden or responsibility is amplified. If you cannot change the circumstances, you may need to change your perspective, or learn to delegate or streamline processes to eliminate time wasting. Others may welcome responsibility, as long as there is financial or career progression. Look at surrounding cards to see whether the hard work will be rewarded. If you have the Hanged Man lurking, nothing will change, and you may still be in the same position in years to come.

Love

Responsibilities or work concerns may cause issues in the love area due to stress. The Ten of Wands is a heavy card, so it dampens any romantic mood. I see this card as the end of a cycle and generally, you might be experiencing a block when this card appears. You could be focusing on the negatives or what's wrong with your love life instead of practicing gratefulness. Know that this too, shall pass.

Health

Feeling a bit down, heavy or tired. This often shows up for sore backs or mobility issues.

As an Outcome Card

The results could put you under pressure or not exactly what you are after. As an outcome card, the path you are following could be a lot of work. It is a block card. Pull a clarifying card if you feel that you need to, and if a further negative card turns up, review your plans. If positive, you will be able to overcome the blocks presented.

ACE OF CUPS

Buzz words: Feeling positive, new beginnings, starting afresh, relaunch, a new opportunity to get going again.

General Meaning

This is a positive card to have appear when you have been feeling down or uninspired or are feeling unloved or unfulfilled. When you draw the Ace of Cups, a new romance or a resurgence of love enters your life. It signifies a new emotional beginning - it can indicate the start of a relationship; whether that be romantic or a friendship. It can indicate hearing positive news that uplifts your mood. As an abstract meaning, this card can indicate creative ideas or starting hobbies or projects. Cups are about emotions and this cup is full of love, hope and inspiration. It may indicate a pregnancy if you have the Empress nearby. Often, the Ace of Cups shows up for new relationships. If you have a run of positive relationship cards such as Two of Cups, Lovers or Hierophant, this may lead to engagement or marriage.

Finances

A new way of dealing with your finances or an opportunity to create more money. There could be a focus on bringing in more money through new ventures.

Career

A new job that gives you greater fulfilment. New projects or roles. You may feel more inspired due to developments or change. You need to remember it is an Ace, and that always denotes something new. You could be looking for inspiration in your career or more expressive outlets.

Love

If you are married or in a relationship, there is a deeper bond developing or a resurgence of love within the relationship. You could have all the giddy feelings you had when you first met. If single, this is a wonderful card to draw to meet someone new and embark on a new relationship. Always look for court cards close by - they will give you information about potential candidates!

Health

You are feeling re-inspired to kick some health goals or try some new tools or modalities to optimize your health. There is a mind/body connection here, so maintain your positivity regarding any health concerns or goals. You may want to reinvent yourself. It is a positive card, so outcomes look positive.

As an Outcome Card

It's a new beginning card, so often it is a Yes card due to its positivity.

TWO OF CUPS

Buzz words: partnerships, love, focus on relationships, respecting others, friendships, agreements, commitment, unity, balance, peace

General Meaning

The Two of Cups is about relationships and unity. It is one of the feel-good cards of deck, as interaction with other people is flowing. It is generally the 'relationship card', but also relates to business partnerships or friendships, so there could be a focus on getting along with others or focusing on love. When this Card appears in a reading, there is more unity within a relationship or a new relationship for singles. It also can relate to the business world, where you might be working with someone. Coming to an agreement is also a buzz term for this card. There is a sense of more peace on the horizon as people are getting on or agreeing.

Finances

Financial agreements, contracts, or money to do with you and other entities could be under the radar. Financial partnerships or working with someone with joint financial goals.

Career

Working with others is amplified - whether that be in a partnership or working closely. There are two energies here getting along and complimenting one another.

Love

The Two of Cups falling within its natural environment of love will heighten relationships, making couples feel more connected. For singles, this is a great card to see if you are searching for love and a relationship. The message would be to keep your heart open. If you have the Lovers Card, Ten of Cups, or Hierophant, it will be a long-lasting relationship.

Health

You may want to work with someone to help you with a health or wellbeing goal to keep you on track or accountable.

As an Outcome Card

As this is a card of agreements, it would be a Yes card.

THREE OF CUPS

Buzz words: good news, positive outcomes, milestones, something to celebrate, events, emotional upliftment, entertainment, drinks, teamwork

General Meaning
The Three of Cups herald's positive outcomes, something to celebrate, events, parties, birthdays, milestones, entertainment or enjoying good food and company.

Finances
Funds could be going out on celebrations or events. You may have a financial win. You may spend some money on a luxury item.

Career
You may socialize with people from work or need to have more fun on the career front. Teamwork or getting along with others could be a key to getting ahead. A need to schmooze with the right people. This is a positive, light-hearted card, so no drama around the career front. You might even just enjoy the social part about going to work or interaction with others at this time.

Love
Romance, dating, having fun, going out and socializing is amplified so take advantage of offers or opportunities to enjoy others' company.

Health

Achieving goals is possible. You'll likely be celebrating some successes but do watch out for over indulging at nights out or events coming up.

As an Outcome Card

It's a celebration card, so yes, enjoy the win or celebrate as there will be good news.

FOUR OF CUPS

Buzz words: Lack of interest, boredom, feeling meh, lack of motivation, apathetic state, an offer that doesn't interest you

General Meaning

The Four of Cups appears when you are bored and unenthusiastic with your lot in life. You could be feeling unmotivated or uninterested with what's going on around you. As a result of this apathetic state, any offers handed to you at this time could seem unappealing. The advice of this card is to take extra time to consider the offer, and whether it is aligned with your goals or desires before knocking it back, and perhaps practice some gratefulness. Life has become stale, so there is a need to look inwards to work out what it is that you want or what will make you happy. For now, you can sit back, but you may miss opportunities if you sit back too long.

Finances

Money matters are not on your priority list right now. Financial offers received are unappealing. Dissatisfaction or feeling glum about your finances.

Career

Bored and uninspired. On the treadmill or doing something because you have to, not because you want to. Job prospects not appealing. Bored silly. Needing new challenges or new direction.

Love

This is a card of having no interest in intimacy due to introspection or boredom. If you are married, you may need to spice things up or if you are dating, it would be suggestive of having lost interest. Self-doubt could be plaguing the relationship area right now. You could be lacking initiative. People in your life are not making an effort

Health

Sitting there doing nothing about your situation. Feeling sorry for yourself or feeling glum. Focusing on all the negatives and not the positives. Hypochondriac.

As an Outcome Card

There won't be an outcome because you will still be sitting there, thinking about things ha-ha. It's a very passive card, so it is a No card. You need to get off your arse and make things happen!

FIVE OF CUPS

Buzz words: Feeling disappointed, hurt, pain, loss, not letting go of the past, wounds

General Meaning

If you chose this card, you need to let go of past hurts, wounds, ex's and disappointment. A need to focus on what we *do* have, not what we don't. Counting your blessings will help you to move forward from being despondent. We can't always win, so just see it as a lesson and heal from this experience. While this is not an overly positive card as it always talks about emotional upsets, the blessing is that healing is possible and this too, shall pass. Don't let worry cloud your judgement. Sometimes rejection or loss is propelling you towards something better. It is a card of emotional grief and it is amplified if you have Swords against it or the Death card where there may have been inevitable change or endings. There is still hope in this card, as two cups are still standing, suggesting that overcoming obstacles is possible, and you still have things in your life to be grateful about.

Finances

Financial upset or loss. If making a financial decision and the Five of Cups appears, it advises you to recheck or guard against potential losses or safe guard yourself. Money issues could bring up disappointment - this could relate to other people and money.

Career

This would be suggestive of feeling disappointed or of unfair decisions being made. A need to let go of words that have wounded your pride or work ethics.

Love

Disappointment around love, reliving wounds from the past, needing to cut energy chords with people from your past, betrayal, hurt, grief.

Health

This card can signify physical pain or issues relating to bleeding or blood. For women, it can signify cycle issues or bleeding. Pop a clarifying card over this one. If you get Ten of Wands or Ten of Swords you will have either back pain or mobility issues, too.

As an Outcome Card

Disappointment

SIX OF CUPS

Buzz words: reminiscing, reunions, old times, celebrations, past, past contacts, people you know, blast from the past, job offers through people you know, networking, daydreaming, childhood

General Meaning

The past is important - whether it's connecting with old colleagues, old friends or even reminiscing about your childhood. There could be a reunion, or you may hear from someone from your past. In the past lies a key to help you right now - whether that be how you successfully handle something, contacting an old colleague or boss, or even an old friend. It's important that we recognize that the past is over and while we may still have fond memories, we also need to live in the now. It's a card full of nostalgia and daydreaming.

Finances

Someone you know may give you sound financial advice or help you in a way that improves your finances.

Career

Skills of the past will prove beneficial to current circumstances. Job offers or assistance coming through past contacts or colleagues you already know. Learn from past mistakes or go over things you did in the past to help you with your current concern. Watch out that you do not daydream on the job.

Love

You may hear from someone from the past. Reminiscing over old times or remembering what you did when you first fell in love could spark romance. For singles, there could be someone from your past returning or an introduction through someone you know. The past is important for a love connection.

Health

An old complaint could resurface. Emotionally, you could be holding onto things from the past that affects your wellbeing. Focus on the now - that is what is important.

As an Outcome Card

The past is important in determining successful outcomes. The message is to utilize your knowledge and contacts to get the desired results. It is a happy card, so the outcome is positive.

SEVEN OF CUPS

Buzz words: confusion, too many options, mind games, all that glistens isn't gold, needing to be realistic, over complicating things, needing to simply things, fantasies

General Meaning

When you draw the Seven of Cups, you are confused due to too many options. You may have wishful thinking or be fantasizing about a matter. This card has several meanings and it's important that you choose the most appropriate for your situation. For example, you are made a ridiculously good offer and it seems too good to be true and you draw the Seven of Cups - the meaning would be all that glistens isn't gold. The advice of the card is to get clear on what you want and eliminate the choices by being realistic and not just looking at the best scenario.

Finances

State of confusion - need to get your shit together! Budget and be realistic about what you can achieve. If a scheme seems too good to be true, it will be just that. You may need to look at all your financial options and make an informed decision by process of elimination.

Career

Often this comes up when we have lots of ideas or options and we don't really know which direction to take. Firstly, eliminate the unsustainable or unrealistic options. Look within yourself to be clear about what it is you really want and see whether those options are a good fit or not. The Seven of Cups often means you may have more than one option. Meditate, ground, or ask a mentor for some advice, as clearly you are too much in your head and could do with a different perspective.

Love

Don't overthink things or over-analyze. While you are in your head analyzing why they said that or did that, you are not in the space of receiving the love you want. On the flip side, if you are single and their profile picture looks like Brad Pitt or Angelina Jolie, you know if it's too good to be true, it's too good to be true. Run now.

Health

Stop Googling *now*. Do not become Dr Google.

As an Outcome Card

Whilst it's not a negative card, it isn't a positive card either, so I would draw a clarifying card. I would take this as a No in itself. You need more clarity.

EIGHT OF CUPS

Buzz words: moving on, leaving behind difficult situations, turning your back, walking away from a relationship or job, walking, back

General Meaning

The Eight of Cups indicates wanting to walk away from a situation; whether that be a job, relationship, or something that you once held dear to your heart, but now causes disappointment and sadness. The Eight of Cups often brings with it major emotional issues, and for this reason you want to walk away from it, rather than resolve it. The pain or loss of enjoyment now overrides any other feelings, and this is usually the quest to a new beginning in finding yourself.

Finances

Exploring new ways to earn income. Feeling unfulfilled materially, walking away with nothing.

Career

Outgrown job or career - time for a change. Current situation is no longer holding the appeal it once had.

Love

Walking away from a relationship or feeling despondent around love and relationships. In search of personal fulfilment.

Health

Walking could be helpful. Look at the imagery of the cards or the keywords - they often will give you insight. This card could also suggest not being happy with a health provider and looking for someone else.

As an Outcome Card

Negative Card so it's energy would bring disappointment.

NINE OF CUPS

Buzz words: emotional fulfilment, happiness, feeling smug (there is a warning of not getting overly confident) wishes and dreams coming true, focus on wellbeing and nutrition, weight gain

General Meaning
Dreams do come true and goals are achieved when the Nine of Cups appears. It is commonly known as the Wish Card, as it brings happiness and fulfilment of your goals and desires.

Finances
Feeling pleased with money situation. Realizing a financial goal. Money could be a driver for fulfilment.

Career
Satisfaction with career direction, so focus on closing off any outstanding matters. As this is a Nine number, we are reminded that before we begin new things, it is important to finish off unfinished projects or any loose ends. The advice with this card in the career sector is to look for job satisfaction.

Love
Cups falling in their natural area will amplify relationships, so you will find connection with others is more flowing and you are feeling more receptive. The Nine of Cups would suggest relationships are happy, but don't get too comfortable and take others for granted. This card suggests counting your blessings.

Health

In terms of health, the focus here is on food and nutrition as being the key elements to tackle. Those calories don't count themselves, those little buggers. It often foretells weight gain in a reading, but please do be mindful of how you deliver this message. On the flip side, focus on the words 'goals' or 'wishes being attained' so if this card is next to positive cards, health is not afflicted, and you can expect good results. Similarly, if you had the Devil or the Three of Cups next to it (party card, you could be overeating or drinking).

As an Outcome Card

Dreams do come true, so it is a yes card.

TEN OF CUPS

Buzz words: Pinnacle of happiness, joy, relationships, happy emotions, home, love, positivity, happy outcomes

General Meaning

The Ten of Cups is the pinnacle card for happiness and indicates that all is well. It is one of the top relationship cards we are looking for in a relationship reading that promises love, family joy, commitment and attainable goals or desires. It is the card of a happy home life and attaining a 'home'. It is a card of harmony and love entering your life. Whatever your concern is about, rest assured that the outcomes are positive and promises love.

Finances

Money matters are looking promising. The word 'home' could be important - whether buying a home or renting -funds may be going towards making your life more comfortable or making decisions around where you want to live. It could also signify investing in things for the home and your future.

Career

Happy times around the career front. You could have the luxury of working from home, or there is a word association with 'home'. Decisions could be based on where you live, or you may have to move because of your job.

Love

Joy and happiness around relationships and being on the same page with your significant other. If times have been troubled, happiness will return. If you are single, expect love to come flowing into your life. Look for court cards close by to give you more information.

Health

If things have been difficult with your health, it shows improvement or feeling happy with developments. Self-nurturing and love are vital ingredients for your emotional wellbeing.

As an Outcome Card

You can expect to be happy or obtain a positive result. It is a Yes card.

ACE OF SWORDS

Buzz words: decisions, clarity, aha moment, discerning, teeth, minor medical, contracts, legal, cutting edge, ideas

General Meaning

Truth, clarity, fresh starts. The Ace of Swords turns up when we are seeking truth, clarity and direction. Its energy is very sharp - we may come to a realization, get that aha moment or make a decision about something important. Being an Ace, it is about new beginnings and is about the power of the mind and taking control over your thoughts. You could get a new idea or be decisive in your thought or direction where previously you were unsure - this is not clouded by emotion it is about thinking things through rationally in order to move forward with plans.

Finances

New ways of making money or following through on an idea to save or optimize finances. Can denote contracts or receiving professional advice with regard to finances. This is about is new beginnings, so apply it to the area of finances, e.g. you may need to look at paperwork for a loan, or work on a budget to achieve a financial goal.

Career

You will obtain the clarity you need to make a fresh start, overcome difficulties or make the necessary career changes. Since this is a communication card, information technology might be a prerequisite, or developed communication skills are necessary to get that job or for advancement. If things have been stale, this brings in new cutting-edge ideas or change.

Love

The word 'truth' is highlighted. If you want to the truth, you need to ask or seek it. It might be *you* revealing a truth. The Ace of Swords is a communication card, and this slices straight through all the bullshit. If you have the Justice card close by with other negative cards, it could mean a break up. It is a cool card and not really what we want in a love reading, however if we are seeking truth for closure, then this is a positive. Don't read the card with its worst interpretation unless other cards close by navigate the story that way. It could simply mean a need to 'clear the air'.

Health

Always denotes medical checkups, dentist or GP visits. Swords are like medical instruments - they seek to find out what's wrong.

As an Outcome Card

Yes, it is a breakthrough card and a new beginning.

TWO OF SWORDS

Buzz words: indecision, minor delays, tension due to unresolved situations, restrictions, a pause, defensive (look at the crossing of arms)

General Meaning

The Two of swords represents a stalemate, a pause or being indecisive. The woman appearing on the card is blindfolded and is unable to make a decision as things are unclear. If you draw the card about developments around something you are hoping to happen, it would indicate minor delays or not hearing back as quickly as you would expect. It is a card of indecision and feeling restricted by your emotional state. It is a standstill card due to an unwillingness of parties to let their guard down, or express ideas or thoughts that would create a breakthrough. On the flip side, this is one of the peaceful cards of this suit due to the feeling of a standstill.

Finances

Delays around financial decisions. Could be feeling restricted financially due to earning capacity. If applying for a loan, there could be minor delays. This card will stall matters or indicate some restriction or barrier to fulfilling a financial goal quickly. The advice of the card is either compromising or finding a solution to work through the stalemate.

Career

This card appearing in the career sector, which indicates going through a slow period where you feel like you are not making progress, and therefore closed off to new ideas or concepts that would allow you to push forward. As a number Two card, it would suggest some tension around work.

Love

You might be not feeling the love if this card shows up in a love reading. Again, you could be feeling defensive or cut off from your emotions. The advice is to get in touch with your feelings and be open to compromise in order to move forward in attracting the love you want, or to have more loving relationships. This card could also represent feeling restricted within a relationship, so you may need to examine how you could obtain more freedom or develop a bigger sense of self.

Health

The blindfold represents issues with the head, so eye strains and headaches are amplified. If followed by the Nine of Swords, could indicate migraine headaches

As an Outcome Card

There is no real progress in this card. You may need to compromise to move forward. It's a stagnation card. Don't give up though - your progress is hindered *temporarily*. It's a No card.

THREE OF SWORDS

Buzz words: Tears, loss. separation, grief, crying, rejection, heart issues, feeling emotional

General Meaning

The Three of Swords image is self-explanatory - a wounded heart that is pierced by three swords with a clouded grey sky representing the heavy atmosphere that surrounds us at this time. When this card appears, tears follow due to rejection, heartbreak, grief or sorrow. This card prewarns us that we could be heading into a difficult time - whether that be a failed relationship, a loss of a job or some other rejection. Look towards surrounding cards to get a sense of the area that's being affected. If close to the Star or Ace of Swords, it could mean some medical procedure in addition to tears, however it does not mean a negative result.

Finances

Arguments over financial affairs. Tears or sadness over not earning enough for your needs, or bills piling up causing you grief. The advice of this card is to accept the financial loss, or where you find yourself and look for new ideas to improve your situation. Money could be going out on health matters.

Career

Arguments or conflict around working life. There is a lack of satisfaction, or things are not going to plan. There is a sense of failure. It is important to remember that this too, shall pass and not to take on the opinions of others unless it's your boss, and if that's the case, you should be examining why he or she is making you so emotional. There is a lack of support when this card appears in the career sector, and you have to shift your focus and think more positively.

Love

Tears and conflict within a relationship. Some readers say this is an affair card because it has three Swords. I see this card as getting into an argument or someone saying something to hurt you. If it was followed by a string of negative cards, such as the Four of Swords, then perhaps a separation or with Five of Cups, Lovers and Seven of Swords, then deception via an affair. It is important that card combos stand out in a reading to give you real information and accuracy. I would not simply state someone is having an affair just by drawing the Three of Swords; that would mean I would have had more affairs than breakfasts!

Health

The Swords do represent medical apparatus, so you could be going to the doctor or dentist for a checkup. With the Three of Swords being a card of tears, your emotional wellbeing could be out of balance and professional support could be helpful at this time.

As an Outcome Card

It's a No Card. Draw a clarifying card if you need to give you further advice, or timing perhaps, for when you could expect a break through or relief from your current concern.

FOUR OF SWORDS

Buzz words: Rest and recuperation, a break, needing time out

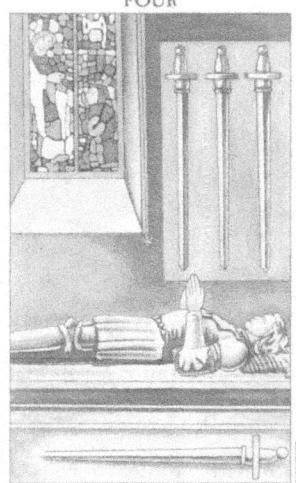

General Meaning

The Four of Swords is a card of rest and recuperation. Sometimes it signifies taking a break off work or not working. It is not a card of death, but rather a time to pause or take some time away from the world to heal, reflect, recuperate or regroup. The answer you are seeking could be to wait until the time is right, or you need to be still in order to hear the answers you need.

Finances

A pause in your financial growth could indeed be caused through lack of work or being unwell. If your question was "will my finances improve?" this would suggest your finances are at a standstill - either through having to take time off work, or things are very slow. It is important to look at the cards next to it to give you an idea of when this idle time will pass. Use this time to think about how you could improve your finances or cut costs. Being an indoors card, it could suggest not to go out as much.

Career

In the career sector, it denotes a slow time, or you are having a break from working. With this card, it shows you may need to bide your time before you are ready to move forward. The phrase, "take a rest, don't quit" comes to mind. If the Hierophant is next to this card, the word 'hospital' is amplified as a place of work or significance. If followed by the Death card, it could be a morgue or places of memorial. With the Four of Wands, you could be going on a holiday - another form of a break from work. The message of this card is to enjoy the rest while you have the downtime; you will be busy enough soon.

Love

Feeling separated or separating from a partner. This card suggests a partner needs space to be alone, reflect, and be in their own energy. Unless you have a string of negative cards, I would not be definite in predicting a divorce or parting of ways. If on the other hand, the Justice card follows, you would expect that a divorce may be imminent. If the client is single, there is not much happening in the love area. Draw a clarifying card to see if the energy changes and give advice accordingly.

Health

Rest and recuperation is amplified with this card being in its natural house of health. If the Hierophant appears, you can expect a hospital visit. If the Knight of Swords follows the Hierophant, then it's a hospital visit by ambulance or rushing to hospital due to pain. If it was an accident, you would see the Tower appear here too.

Such combos can also relate to emergency workers which could be the client's occupation. I recently saw this combo in my own reading and I had to rush my husband to hospital as he got a nail through his foot. It showed me a foot in the three images, so I knew it would be someone's foot.

It's important to note that you have a duty of care and I'm teaching tarot combos for your *learning*. Readings should empower people, not instill fear or plant a seed. I am simply showing you how we blend cards to give them real meanings. Never, ever predict a death or say to someone that they will have an accident.

As an Outcome Card

It is a No Card. You won't make much headway at this time. Use this time to regroup, rest and trust that things will happen in the right timing.

FIVE OF SWORDS

Buzz words: conflict, strife, win at all costs, defeating, defeat, competition, arguments, litigation

General Meaning

The appearance of the Five of Swords brings conflict, tension, competition or strife - there is a sense of having a fight on your hands. Although the message of the card is defeat over the opposition or obtaining what you want, there is no real winner here as someone has lost or it has come at some cost. There is another message here about picking your battles as being a much more peaceful way of living. It is a challenging card and sometimes things come to a head, but the energy surrounding the victory seems somewhat hollow.

Finances

Disagreements around money or financial concerns. You could be feeling defensive about what you earn or don't earn.

Career

Tension or competition around the work front. A need to pick your battles as you do not want to get others offside. Colleagues could be argumentative or divided over ideas. Clients could be demanding.

Love

Take care that you don't get into tit for tat type of discussions that lead to an argument or tension. If single, you may feel there is a lot of competition out there. Remember that we all have someone out there for us - don't give up hope.

Health

Walking could be beneficial for your health. Watch your back area.

As an Outcome Card

Shallow victory due to either all the hassle involved, or conflict, but it's still a win - depends on how you see it. The advice of the card is to pick your battles, or if you follow this path, weighing up who it affects or how you still maintain relationships while pursuing goals. It's a card that needs navigation.

SIX OF SWORDS

Buzz words: trip, moving, moving on, calm after storm, calmer waters, feeling more settled, clarity, thinking rationally, acceptance, realization

General Meaning
When the Six of Swords appears, one can expect to sail into calmer waters, things settle down and a sense of peace prevails. This card is suggestive of earlier turmoil following on from the Five of Swords.

The Six of Swords reminds us to look forward and let go of any past disputes or anything that does not bring us peace. With peace, brings healing. There is always a tinge of sadness associated with this card about having to move on from something - whether that be a job, home, or another situation - but you know it's for the best. It is a card about gaining clarity and moving past your emotions to deal with what you need to do regarding future plans. It is a card you want to see regarding moving on or healing from any issue or concern. It is also about accepting the truth about your situation. It is a movement card and often denotes trips.

Finances
Overcoming financial concerns, paying or saving for a trip.

Career
Transitioning or moving, overcoming conflict, opportunities from interstate or afar.

Love

Feeling calmer or being able to rationalize how you are feeling or seeing things from another's perspective. Peace following arguments.

Health

This is a card of healing as you move on from what is troubling you and look positively towards the future. Going on a trip may help you to heal.

As an Outcome Card

It is a movement card, so it is a Yes.

SEVEN OF SWORDS

Buzz words: dodgy emails, accounts hacked, lies, gossip, questioning if someone can be trusted, feeling cautious, deceit

General Meaning

The Seven of Swords is the deceit, lie, dodgy information and scammers card. The swords are associated with communication, so you may hear something where you are questioning someone's agenda, you may question if it is true, or you may question the integrity of the information. The Seven of Swords can also relate to people copying your ideas or gossiping about you. The Seven of Swords can indicate lack of communication, misjudgment and needing to trust your gut instincts as something feels off. In any case, it is suggestive of keeping your cards close to your chest and to sit back before you jump to conclusions or get involved. Trust your gut instincts - if you feel someone is playing mind games, they probably are.

If you have some ideas for your work or plans, keep your mouth shut. Now, it's not all bad; it is school yard stuff, but it could still annoy you. The Seven of Swords can create some anxiety when it appears, so be mindful not to allow the action of others to take away your peace of mind. If next to the Magician, it can amplify anxiety, so extra care is needed if this combo appears in a reading.

Finances

This card can describe uncertainty around income flow. Often, it comes up for people who are self-employed, or work casually or part time. There is a sense of having flexibility with your time, but it comes with uncertainty with when the next pay check or amount comes in. Should the Moon fall next to it within a finance question, watch out for scammers or check/re-check that you have correct information. This card warns you to be on guard. You could get ripped off by a client or someone could take advantage of you in a financial way. If followed by the Three of Pentacles, it may indicate break-ins or theft. If followed by the Page of Swords, someone could steal your ideas so again, try to keep things close to your chest at this time.

Career

The Seven of Swords gives off uncertainty - whether that be in direction or job security. This card appearing within the context of a career reading would guide you to be wary and ask questions, but don't jump to conclusions. If you are suspecting someone has an agenda, it would confirm your suspicion to be true. Colleagues could steal your ideas, or you may have copy right issues. On the flip side, if you are looking for a part time role, this would confirm it is part time compared to full time. Next to the Justice card, it would give you the word 'injustice', as the Seven of Swords diminishes the fairness of the Justice card. If you were looking to change jobs, it could be a temporary move as opposed to a long term one.

Love

The Seven of Swords is definitely not a card you want to see in a love reading, as it brings up trust issues, lies or possible infidelity. Before you accuse someone of infidelity however, you would really want the Devil, Moon, Five of Cups and Lovers appearing, too. In itself, without the issue of affairs, trust could be an issue in the relationship due to the past. Remember, you have duty of care in a reading, so it's important to deliver difficult news delicately. You do not know what state of mind the client is in.

Health

I often see this card appearing in readings for passing medical issues. In other words, the word is 'temporary'. This card also relates to anxiety as it's a very edgy card and if next to the Devil or Magician, can amplify dealing with depression and or anxiety. The message to be delivered is to seek help and that you are never alone. Whatever is troubling you will pass.

As an Outcome Card

This card does not bring long term stability. It should be seen either as a stepping stone or a temporary solution or situation. It is a No card, due to the uncertainty it brings. I would draw a clarifying card to confirm.

EIGHT OF SWORDS

Buzz words: self-sabotaging, feeling powerless, lacking confidence, insecure, doubt, hesitant

General Meaning

The Eight Swords turns up when we have sabotaging thoughts, are feeling restricted, or lacking confidence. This is the 'Negative Nancy' card - the little nagging, whiny voice we hear in our heads, telling us how bad things are, why we can't do something, and thinking the worst. The upside to this card is that our self-defeating thoughts can be changed, and we need to nip them in the bud. It is not the truth of the matter; is it only our perception. The number 8 is about power, so you have power over your thoughts and therefore, over your outcomes. You could be feeling powerless or not being able to see the solution to your current concern, or you may be refusing to see the truth of the matter. The picture of the bound lady reminds us to use our Swords (our logical thoughts and rational mind) to cut through the bondage that keeps us trapped.

Finances

The bills are piling up or you are worrying about how you are going to pay for something. There is a feeling of restriction or not being able to move forward with financial goals or plans. The advice of this card is to stop fueling the worry and direct your energy into being proactive or finding solutions that would minimize your expenses or new ways of optimizing income.

Career

The energy concerning work or around work could be negative, and self-doubt could be creeping in. Victimization or bullying could be shaking your confidence. You could be feeling trapped in what you do and if followed by the Devil, it amplifies staying in a job for security because it pays the bills, but it is killing your soul.

Love

The Eight of Swords describes how one is feeling either within a relationship, or how they are relating to others. It brings up insecurities, a lack of confidence and feeling negative. Watch out for projecting unhappiness onto another. Happiness is an inside job - no one is going to rescue you.

Health

The card of the hypochondriac, Googling every ailment. Stop worrying. You should be more worried about the obsessiveness than the ailment. If you are worried about a health concern, the quicker you have it looked at, the better, but this card is generally your own fear coming. Headaches or eye issues.

As an Outcome Card

It's a No card

NINE OF SWORDS

Buzz words: worry, nightmares, depression, sleepless nights, broken sleep, anguish, overwhelm, uncertainty

General Meaning

Try to stop worrying. Worrying about this and worrying about that could be consuming you. Instead, trust in the process of life and that things have a way of working out. Don't let the worry overwhelm you - you are making yourself sick with the worry - even to the point of having broken sleep. If you have the Moon and the Devil close by, nightmares could be causing you anguish. The Nine of Swords appearing often reflects our fear of future outcomes which are based on our internal fears, not the actual reality or outcome as such. The Law of Attraction however, would encourage us to focus on being more positive, so we attract more positive life experiences.

Finances

Money or long-term security could be a concern. Worrying about the future has become obsessive in nature, causing you anguish. This card could indicate that you need to make some changes to your financial affairs in order to alleviate your worry levels.

Career

The career sector could be putting you under a lot of pressure and stress. If court cards fall close by, this would indicate who it may be that's giving you grief or causing that worry. The advice of this card is that your own thoughts could be fueling the situation at hand, and a need to put things into perspective. Remember it is a 9 number, so the situation will come to an end soon. Don't give up or give into your thoughts.

Love

If you are in a relationship, you may enter a testing stage where you may think the worst or wonder where it is going. Perhaps you are worried about your partner. Your thoughts are worse than the reality. If you don't have a run of negative cards, I would not be calling the solicitor. If single, the energy in finding someone suitable is currently subzero. There is nothing lining up at the moment, however, don't despair. Have a chocolate fix - it doesn't talk back! Look at rewording your affirmations or love intentions. It will happen; there is someone for everyone.

Health

Worry and anxiety is causing you broken sleep or sleepless nights. You could be worrying about a health concern or your wellbeing. It is important that you face your fears or get to the root of the problem. Our fears are often worse at night and it is important to remember that all we need to fear is fear itself. This is mainly a card about worry and fear and it often does not represent the reality of a situation but rather our thoughts.

As an Outcome Card

It's not a positive card, so it's a No. Just remember though, it is a fear-based card, so it is usually your own fear coming up.

TEN OF SWORDS

Buzz words: Difficult time, ending, stagnation, backstabbed, sore back or pain

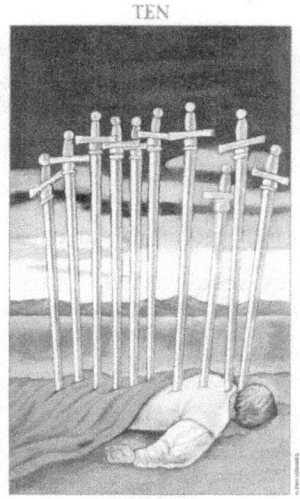

General Meaning

The Ten of Swords indicates difficult experiences associated with endings or going through change which can be challenging. The upside is that you are at the end of a cycle and you *will* get through this. It is Minor version of the Death Card in some respects - it does cause tears as a result of the anguish suffered, but it will end soon. If it follows the Death card, it often means we are hanging on for dear life or not wanting to go with the flow - change is inevitable. The pain of this card is about fighting against the change and not going with the flow. Once you can surrender and accept the lesson of the situation, you can move on and the anguish is often released.

Finances

As this is the end of a cycle, you could be looking at ways to finalize debt arrangements or renew finance arrangements. I use this card as a measure stick to give me the word 'cycle'. This could translate to periodic payments. It is a negative card, so if your question was 'will my finance improve?' it would be not at the moment, or you need to implement some change to improve cashflow, etc.

Career

Most readers identify this card as being stabbed in the back, so watch out for political games or competition. When this appears for a career reading, it can feel like foretelling gloom and doom. If difficult cards surround it, the client will end up leaving work as you cannot sustain this energy for too long. The Ten of Swords with Five of Pentacles and Tower would equal job loss. If it has positive cards close by, adversity will be overcome, but if you have a string of negative cards, it would suggest something coming to a head.

Love

A relationship going through a significant rough period. This is just not the squabbles of the Five of Wands - the wounds and words used cut much deeper. Can the partnership survive? If single, don't give up - try a different platform to meet people or take a break from it, however this is the end of a cycle, so be prepared for changes.

Health

I often see this in readings for back pain or suffering pain. This then, is predictive of having to use professional medical services to improve your health.

As an Outcome Card

It's a No card.

ACE OF PENTACLES

Buzz words: money coming in, things coming together, stability, circle of friends, feeling supported, new beginnings, loans, lump sums, stability

General Meaning

The Ace of Pentacles promises new beginnings that have financial benefits. Financial increases, things finally coming together, loans, settlements, new beginnings that have a financial impact, and job offers are all buzzwords associated with this card. When the Ace of Pentacles appears, it reassures us that our financial concerns will improve, as will our security and stability. Working hard and steadily will pay off.

Finances

Loans are granted, and money increases are expected when this card shows up. It is not a win unless it has the Wheel of Fortune or the Six of Pentacles beside it; with the latter likely being gifted. If the Ten of Pentacles is close by, you may receive money through family or an inheritance. You can expect to feel more stable in the financial department. Lump sums also come under the radar. This could be doing work for lump sums or could be you receiving a lump sum due to a settlement.

Career

New beginnings around work, offers, projects. Feeling like you have come full circle. Changes.

Love

Feeling one with your partner or being on the same page, feeling supported. For singles, it may indicate joining groups, clubs or places where there are likeminded people, and it could be fun.

Health

Gyms and places of group settings are highlighted for health improvements.

As an Outcome Card

Things will come together. It is a positive card.

TWO OF PENTACLES

Buzz words: Juggling, two sources of income, up and down

General Meaning

The Two of Pentacles is a card of juggling finances and it's a balancing act. It is not a card of financial worry, despite the fact you may need to juggle your income around. You can be very resourceful as this often indicates two income streams or money to be made from another source. It is a card of more balance entering your life and the ability to adapt to change. If you look at the man in the picture, he is holding the Pentacles in the shape of the infinity symbol, which brings hope and inspiration. When this card appears, you may need to priorities or better manage your time. You could have two jobs or two roles, or you may be juggling study with work, or even between motherhood and playing another important role.

Finances

If finances have been tight, there are more funds coming in, however, this is not a card of riches, as money often goes out paying expenses and overheads. Often, we need to balance our bank accounts or books, or ensure we pay our bills on time when this card appears. If you have an idea about earning income, scope it out - it could provide another income stream.

Career

This card often appears when we are doing more than one thing. We could have our own business while still having another job to supplement the income. Another possibility is that you could be performing two roles at work - if the Ten of Wands follows, it would suggest an unrealistically high workload, or you are under pressure. This card asks you to manage your time and prioritize. There is a big focus on juggling, so it is important whether that be study, job, or family that you adapt a balanced approach to everything. You can't be everything to everyone all at the one time.

Love

Being the card of balance, it is important that you adapt in relationships and also prioritize what is important. If relationships have been strained, this card would suggest that more balance will flow in due to going with the flow or making your loved one a priority. On the flip side, if you are single, are you weighing up your options?

Health

This card is about balance, so the guidance is balancing work and life commitments so that you can focus on your health goals. The word balance could be important in health matters when you need to balance hormones.

As an Outcome Card

This card brings in more balance, or situations stabilize. You may have more than one option.

THREE OF PENTACLES

Buzz words: financial increase, collaboration, mastering a skill, mentoring, promotion, recognition, shops, venues, tradies, renovations, working towards goals, mastery of one's trade

General Meaning
The Three of Pentacles is about financial growth through collaboration or help from others. It highlights working with others to learn or grow, and to help master techniques and skills. It is the card for teamwork as a key to improve your financial position. Collaborations of all sorts come under this card and it is imperative that clear communication and boundaries are implemented so it doesn't affect the atmosphere or workflow. You may be mentored or are mentoring. Shops, venues, restaurants or places of interest are highlighted as revenue earning ideas.

Finances
Money flow is improving. You may be thinking of spending on home improvements, renovations or purchasing items to decorate your spaces.

Career
Working as a team or looking at it from a team point of view is important. Recognition of skills or discussions about promotions in line with skill sets are amplified. With the Magician next to this card, it would translate to a team leader. There could be a venture where you are collaborating with another person or business. It is a card of advancement.

Love

Improvement for married couples, however you may need to inject more fun into the relationship. For singles, take the opportunity to go out have fun - you never know who you may meet while you are out (this is the Tradie card - you may want to venture to your local hardware store ha-ha).

Health

You may need support from health professionals or others to help you achieve your goals, but it shows progress.

As an Outcome Card

It is a positive card and is suggestive that others may help you with achieving a goal or a desired result.

FOUR OF PENTACLES

Buzz words: money coming in, security, stability, normal results, going to be okay, trust that the future will take care of itself

General Meaning

The Four of Pentacles arrives to let us know that we are safe, secure and there is stability for the future. You may be striving towards financial security or focusing on bricks and mortar - know that what you are hoping for the future will come to fruition. If you have been worried about something, everything is going to be okay. Try not to focus too much on having enough money or focusing on the future, as you will miss out on the moment of here and now.

Finances

More money coming in, focusing on security or something solid for the future, savings. If the Devil is next to it, someone could be holding onto their money or being miserly.

Career

Solid career choices in the pipeline or a sense of acceptance or permanency around vocation. If there has been worry around career, it will be sorted out. Getting into a routine or setting up new processes may help you to achieve more. If you have felt uncertain about job security, reassurance is given.

Love

Dependability and reliability may be buzzwords here that connect to love. For singles, actions speak louder than words and the words 'commitment' or 'long-term' may be what you are seeking. Don't give up; someone just like you is out there.

Health

Improvements, normal, needing to get into routines to sustain health goals.

As an Outcome Card

It is a positive card that assures a secure future. It is a number 4 card, which provides structure and stability.

FIVE OF PENTACLES

Buzz words: Money problems, feeling left out in the cold, Money losses or being out of work

General Meaning
The Five of Pentacles turns up when we are feeling despondent about our financial affairs, have lost faith in our relationships, or just in ourselves. There is a feeling of being left out in the cold as depicted by the card itself, which translates to the fear of being out on the road if money matters or relationships don't improve. It can point to a time when life is less than secure. The important thing to remember is that there is always help available, whether that is financial assistance or relationship counselling. If you were asking whether a job move was the right choice, and this showed up, it would indicate that you could soon be looking again for another job. It often foretells hardship or struggle and while there are definitely negative connotations around this card, there is still hope within this card that if you open the door and ask for help, you'll receive it while you get back on your feet.

Finances
It does indicate financial loss, however, consider which card appears close by. For example, if the Tower appears, you could unexpectedly throw in your job, be made redundant or suffer a financial blow, such as bankruptcy. It does warn you to keep an eye on your financial affairs and minimize outlays.

Career

Feeling lost, no sense of direction or unemployed. You could be feeling on the outer or not in the flow of your life, calling or path when the Five of Pentacles appears. The message of not giving up, asking for help when things get too tough emotionally, is also a message to remember. Draw a clarifying card to see when things will improve or for further guidance.

Love

This is a no brainer - not feeling the love in a relationship or feeling tension. Sometimes this comes up when we are waiting to hear from someone or they choose to withdraw their energy. There is also a sense of missing someone. This is one of the 'bad' relationship cards, as the connection has been lost. The advice of the card is to ask whether you need closure or open communication to clear up unresolved issues? If you are single and if you are wondering if he/she is the one, keep searching those profiles or keep your options open.

Health

This card for health would mean not feeling well, run down or getting a cold. You may need to look after your health more in the coming weeks.

As an Outcome Card

Sorry, you are not going to be happy with the outcome.

SIX OF PENTACLES

Buzz words: charity, non-profit, generosity, bonuses, settlements, energy exchange, gifts, thyroid, groups, circles

General Meaning

This is the card of energy exchanges - giving and receiving. On one hand, you may be giving and feeling short changed, but you may find that energy whether that be in the form of money or emotional support, will come from somewhere else. Regardless of when this card appears, there will be a focus on what you are giving to others and reflecting on what you are receiving from another. It can be a paradoxical card that asks us to examine the polarity of situations; our gains and losses, and what we are hoping to achieve from being kind or giving. It asks you to examine your underlying motive. It is the card of small wins or gifts, financial improvements or paying it forward.

Finances

The Six of Pentacles being a money card, denotes money improvements. It often appears for settlements; especially if the Justice card and/or Hierophant are close by, as it would infer large organizations or government departments are involved. Could also mean payouts from insurance companies. You could also be giving to charity or paying it forward.

Career

As a career option, non-profit or charity organizations could be a focus, or an opportunity to work in such an organization. This card suggests working in roles where you are helping those in need, as opposed to a commercial environment. This may not reflect the culture but describes the organization. If you had the Death card, Moon and Six of Pentacles - working in cancer research or for a cancer charity organization. If you had the Hanged Man appearing with the Six of Pentacles, your life work could be research or volunteering. The Six of Pentacles is about being of service.

Love

The Six of Pentacles appearing for a relationship reading could bring up power issues within the relationship. Is someone investing more time and energy than the other? Who is holding the power? If the Seven of Swords appears next to this card, you could become resentful if you feel the other party is not giving equally. You may need to step back and assess why power games are happening, or what you need to learn from it. Do things because you want to, not to buy love or approval.

Health

There is a message here about optimizing your health through making lifestyle changes. Because it is a card of balance, look to balance your hormones.

As an Outcome Card

It is a positive card for financial gain, or a win of some sort.

SEVEN OF PENTACLES

Buzz words: Slow growth, time for reflection, hard work will pay off eventually, need to look at long term goals, long term investments, water your garden, tend to business matters

General Meaning

Patience is needed when this card appears. You may be feeling frustrated that things are not happening as quickly as you would like. It is a time to reflect, prepare, and organize before you take action, so things moving slowly is actually working for you, as it allows you to think about your direction more carefully. It is a time to rest and withdraw, knowing that prosperity is coming your way, but that things just take time. Always think about progress like attending to a garden - you have many elements such as seasons and having to tend and wait for the harvest. There are reasons for delays and blocks, even if we don't quite understand them at the time. It's just about accepting where you find yourself and letting go and trusting in the process of life.

The Seven of Pentacles always appears when you feel you deserve to be further ahead than where you find yourself. Just let it go, or it will do your head in. See it as a time to review where you have been and prepare where you are going, and then just trust. Practice some grounding, get back into the present moment, and shift your focus off progress. Feed your soul with something that inspires you.

Finances

Slow growth but making solid progress. The hard work and investment will pay off long term, but you need to view it from a long-term perspective. Investing in your own business.

Career

Although this card talks about slow growth, there is a message to evaluate how far you have come and to assess where to from here. Take the time while things seem a bit slow, to take stock and reflect where or what next. You could be thinking about your own business or how to advance in your career. The message is the same: you will reap the rewards of your hard work.

Love

The Seven of Pentacles within the context of a love reading asks you to reflect on the growth or direction of your relationship. On the flip side, it can be making you ask, "is my relationship going anywhere?". It's time to evaluate what you want out of relationships and love.

Health

Slow results around health goals, however if you put the hard work in, it will pay off. It is important to understand that it could take time and effort to accomplish things. This would indicate slow progress; however, you need to remind yourself how far you have come and that things take time.

As an Outcome Card

Hard work will pay off, but you must hang in there.

EIGHT OF PENTACLES

Buzz words: diligence, getting on with it, courses, learning, aptitude, perseverance paying off, workshops, accreditation, exams, certificates, apprentice

General Meaning

The Eight of Pentacles is an 8 card, so it does mean success with work and financial endeavors. The energy of the Eight of Pentacles will see one work toward goals, confirming that hard work will pay off, that finances will improve, and that issues can be sorted out practically. This is a card of knowing your shit, working hard and getting ahead. This is also the card of learning, trades, courses and accreditation, so perhaps this is a path to pursue.

Finances

Creating wealth and financial improvement is under the radar, and this is achieved through hard work and application. You could be investing in accreditation or further learning. Book work or accounting matters could need your attention.

Career

You know your stuff, so do not doubt yourself. Learning, courses, accreditation, and certificates could help your resume. Hard work and applying yourself will pay off. Training others could be something you are good at.

Love

Working out issues practically and logically. It's not a terribly romantic card, but it is suggestive of needing to focus more on the area of relationships.

Health

Starting health plans, reviewing goals, having tests maybe on the radar, but you will get there.

As an Outcome Card

It is positive, but suggestive of needing to keep working at it. As an 8 number, it heralds success, but you must work for it. It doesn't come without sweat.

NINE OF PENTACLES

Buzz words: financial improvements, feeling comfortable where things are at, but needing further excitement or a challenge, financial investments

General Meaning

When the Nine of Pentacles appears, you are feeling comfortable where things are at, harvesting the fruits of your labor, or seeing your time and investments paying off. This is a money card, which shows improvement coming where you have done the work - the hard work will pay off. There is also a message of cashing into something that you may have put a lot of work or money into, but not done anything with lately. There is money to be made from old investments. Before you move onto a new project, remember this is a Nine card, and there is money to be made from something from the past.

Finances

Drawing money cards in the money area is a big sigh of relief as finances improve or the flow of abundance switches back on. You could be making some sound financial decisions at this time.

Career

Feeling comfortable where things are at, but you will soon be ready for your next challenge. You may feel you deserve a pay rise, or you could be using your experience as a leverage for more money. You could be sitting pretty with what you're doing right now. Take a rest; you have earned it. Things may change soon enough.

Love

Entering a phase in your love life where you are comfortable being yourself. You are entering a more enriching and loving phase in your life where there is no drama. If you are currently having issues in the love department the Nine of Pentacles is suggesting being comfortable in your own skin and that you will be accepted. The buzzword here is feeling "comfortable" or being in a good place.

Health

Don't get too comfortable. You need to shake it up.

As an Outcome Card

It's a positive card, so whatever is on your mind has a positive outcome. It is within your reach.

TEN OF PENTACLES

Buzz words: Family home, assets, inheritance, family life, self-employment or family business, wealth, property

General Meaning

When this card appears, there will be a focus on long term plans such as mortgages or property. You could be discussing wills, estates, superannuation so that you can pass this onto later generations. It is the card of financial stability so if things have been a worry, know that plans you are putting in place will be good long-term investments or prospects. It is also a card about home and family, so you could be supporting your family or there is a focus on your family life. It is a positive card and augurs financial growth and a sense of stability in your life.

Finances

Mortgages, wills. Estates, financial planning is highlighted. This card shows making long term decisions around money matters. It always denotes material success

Career

In the career sector this often falls for self-employed people or working for a family company. This card is the highest denomination in the pentacles series, so you can expect financial increases around work. It can also suggest secure employment as it has connotations of long term.

Love

As this is a solid long-term card as an outcome card for a love question, this would suggest that someone would want to commit to you or go to the next step. You could be accepted by your significant other's family. It is a long-term partner commitment card. You could be buying property together or joining bank accounts. There is this sense of becoming family.

Health

When this card appears in the health area, often people have fears about hereditary diseases. While we need to be vigilant and do what we can by addressing with the appropriate health providers, there is also a message of not getting consumed by it either. In this position, this card could suggest you are worried about someone's health in the family or something passed down. Stop worrying and obtain medical advice. This card would suggest you will be around for a long time.

Outcome Card: Yes, positive financial outcomes, happy family life.

Blending or Linking Cards

Blending or Linking Cards - An Alternative to Reversals

Whilst I do not read reversals, I have included a list at the back of the book for quick reference should you wish to learn a key word or two. It is a personal choice. My own theory is that there are enough challenging cards in the deck to heighten or diminish the meaning of cards that are close by. You will find your own way to read tarot, as there are no right or wrong ways. Be guided by your own feelings as to whether you want to read reversals, or just blend the cards or read card combos to give you more information about people and situations.

Example 1: Three of Cups, The Devil, The Moon

There may be some concern around someone's drinking habits - they could be overindulging. Or, if this does not relate to you, it may relate to someone close that affects you. You may be in denial about this, but deep down it may be troubling you with how much you're consuming. If you are addicted, take steps to overcome this dependency before it takes over your life.

You or someone close is hanging around the wrong crowd and as a result, this could feed the addiction. A need to really examine things and trust your intuition here, as things are not what they seem.

Explanation

Firstly, the Devil jumps out at me, as it is a Major Arcana card and quite negative in its associations. I immediately saw an issue regarding some form of control, addiction or entrapment. The Devil deals with bad habits, negativity, addictions, excessive materialism, toxic relationships and unhealthy living and attitudes. The Devil may also relate to unhealthy relationships or friendships. The Three of Cups with the Devil next to it tells me that these 'friends' do not have the client's best interest at heart. The temptation becomes too strong and the lure is there for them to give in, as they are seduced back to what has become an addiction or at the very least, a very bad habit. And so, the cycle continues, and the individual becomes more and more powerless.

Look across to The Moon. This person knows deep down that they are in trouble and this concern has begun to surface more and more, to the extent that it is deeply troubling them. They know they are in trouble as their subconscious calls to them. They may be beginning to understand that the deep issues or emotions they are trying to suppress with alcohol, drugs, food, sex etc. are still managing to rise up and make themselves known. Their issues have probably become worse, and it is for certain that their self-esteem is plummeting. The Moon is their wake-up call, for they are beginning to acknowledge their worries and concerns regarding the way they are living and are gaining an understanding of where it all has come from.

For me, these cards would suggest that the individual is close to reaching the point where depression and self-loathing will make them begin to turn away from The Devil (addiction, substance etc.) as they realize this path is not serving them. This path is toxic and self-destroying. Through linking these cards, you can see that this is a serious situation that needs the client to find inner strength to battle their demons and process their subconscious feelings in a way that empowers them, and not make them a slave to their addictions. At this point, you would suggest that counseling may assist with this situation. You build a story from connecting the cards.

Example 2: The Devil and Strength
The patience found in the Strength card is diminished by the Devil next to it, as the Devil makes you feel powerless and trapped. The Strength card is an energy and health card, but with Devil, it would tell you that your energy is sapped. In other words, the Devil or the challenging card will diminish the positivity of the card next to it, so you

can bring through the appropriate message. It could also mean that you need to take your pet to the vet, as the Strength card covers animals.

Example 3: The Sun and Strength

Good health and vitality. The Sun shines down on you. The Strength card is exalted with the positivity and radiance of the sun. Health improves, or patience pays off.

Example 4: The Devil and The Magician

The positivity of the Magician and the opportunities it normally brings with this card combo now becomes 'opportunistic' or the traits 'controlling' or 'narcissistic'. This could be someone in a position of power that can exploit people.

Example 5: The Magician, The Emperor, Justice

A judge or barrister.

The Magician makes him a leader or specialist in his field. The Emperor is 'Top Dog' and Justice refers to the legal system

Example 6: Justice, Eight of Swords

Imprisonment or working in a prison.

Example 7: The Empress, King of Swords

Gynecologist. The Empress represents our fertility and the King of Swords is often a doctor.

Example 8: The Magician, King of Swords

A specialist. If we had an oncologist, in addition we would see the Moon and Death cards. A heart surgeon with the Three of Swords in addition to the specialist combo.

I could go on and on, but you get the gist of building up a tarot vocabulary through linking cards and card combos.

Rephrasing Questions

Rephrasing Questions

By asking open ended questions, it allows the person to be responsible for their own actions as they have free will and it is an empowering way to work with the Tarot. I am not going to deny that sometimes things are very definitive in the reading, and that could mean seeing a new job or the end of a relationship, however, you have a duty of care to disclose this information in the most caring way possible, as you do not know your client's state of mind. Always make the person feel empowered; that they have choices and it's not all gloom and doom, without compromising the information you receive during the reading.

Examples of rephrasing questions

Will I end up with Mr. Big?
What do I need to know about my relationship with Mr. Big?

Will I get a new job?
What do I need to do to get a new job?

Is my husband having an affair?
What do I need to know about my relationship? Where is my relationship heading?

Do I have a serious health problem?
What can I do to improve my health and wellbeing?

CARD SPREADS

Spreads

The accuracy of your reading will be dependent on a few things including which spread you use. For Yes/No readings, don't do a big spread, as you will get lost in the detail. Use either a two-card or a four-card spread (maximum). You can initially do a general spread to get a feel about the situation, however if you want a quick answer, stick to very basic spreads.

You can make up your own spreads to suit questions, or rewrite ones in words that mean something to you. I find some of the relationship spreads quite encumbersome. Choose ones that are simple and don't have too many positional meanings, as you will not remember them. When learning, an idea is to use an A3 artist pad, draw cards and write the positional meanings under the cards so it allows you to place your real tarot card on the blank tarot card image, so then you can read the positional meaning.

I have shared some of my favorite spreads in this book. You will work out which you feel comfortable reading. You can write your own spreads in words that make sense to you.

TAROT CELTIC SPREAD

5. Crown Card
Attitude and belief
about the matter

10. Outcome

1. Current Circumstances

9. Hopes

4. Immediate Past
How it influenced the
matter, or how it was.

2. Challenge Card
What is crossing
your path?

6. Immediate Future
Read this in
conjunction with
#10 outcome card.

**8. How others
see you**
Family resources,
opinions

**3. The past and how it
influenced the matter.**

7. What you fear

Choose your significator based on
Star Sign if you wish to do so.
This may help you to focus.

Choose your significator. If you wish to do so based on star sign, this may help you to focus.

1. Current circumstances
2. Challenge card - what is crossing your path?
3. The past and how it influenced the matter
4. Immediate past - how this influenced the matter at hand, or how it was
5. Crown card - attitude and belief about the matter
6. Immediate future- read this in conjunction with number 10 outcome card
7. What you fear
8. How others see you/family resources/opinions
9. Hopes
10. Outcome

Example Celtic Spread Reading
Question: "What does work look like?"

Card 1: Current circumstances (Three of Pentacles) *You have the skills necessary to get a job that is in line with your experience. You are a team player and that will work for you.*

Card 2: Challenge card - what is crossing your path? (Four of Swords) *The Four of Swords is talking about a period, like a block period of not working, or waiting patiently for a job to come your way. Acceptance of your situation and allowing for healing is necessary at the moment. Don't fight it.*

Card 3: The past and how it influenced the matter (Four of Pentacles) *You have always gone for job security, so you are looking for security and stability in your job prospects.*

Card 4: Immediate past - how this influenced the matter at hand, or how it was (The Star) *The Star suggests that you are positive and look for the best outcomes, and this positivity will hold you in good stead.*

Card 5: Crown card - attitude and belief about the matter (Nine of Cups) *Prospects are looking good. You will fulfil your work goals and feel pleased with your progress. Your attitude is extremely positive, and the Law of Attraction will tell you that you will attract more blessings.*

Card 6: immediate future- read this in conjunction with number 10 outcome card (King of Wands) *This card always talks about dynamic energy and things moving ahead. A male could be helpful in you obtaining a role. This talks about getting out there and negotiating and putting ideas into action. With this position, also look at the outcome card, which is The Sun, so I feel that a fire sign male or a very entrepreneurial type male will cross your path and assist you with job prospects.*

Card 7: What you fear (Six of Pentacles) *You are a very giving person and know that you would give 116%. You may want to ensure that your worth is acknowledged through negotiating a reasonable agreement. You may fear that you will not get paid enough for the role, or expectations are too high in comparison to remuneration.*

Card 8: How others see you/family resources/opinions (Two of Swords) *With the Two of Swords, it could mean that you may be tense during this time. I also see this position as family. and tensions could arise due to how you feel about loss of employment or looking for employment. Feelings of having to wait due to delays and having to stall things around the home, or things to do with family.*

Card 9: Hopes (Seven of Swords) *Wanting flexibility*

Card 10: Outcome (The Sun) *Great outcome, despite having to wait. The Sun shines on you and the wait is worth it. Positive outcomes and being able to negotiate something that works for you.*

QUESTION SPREAD

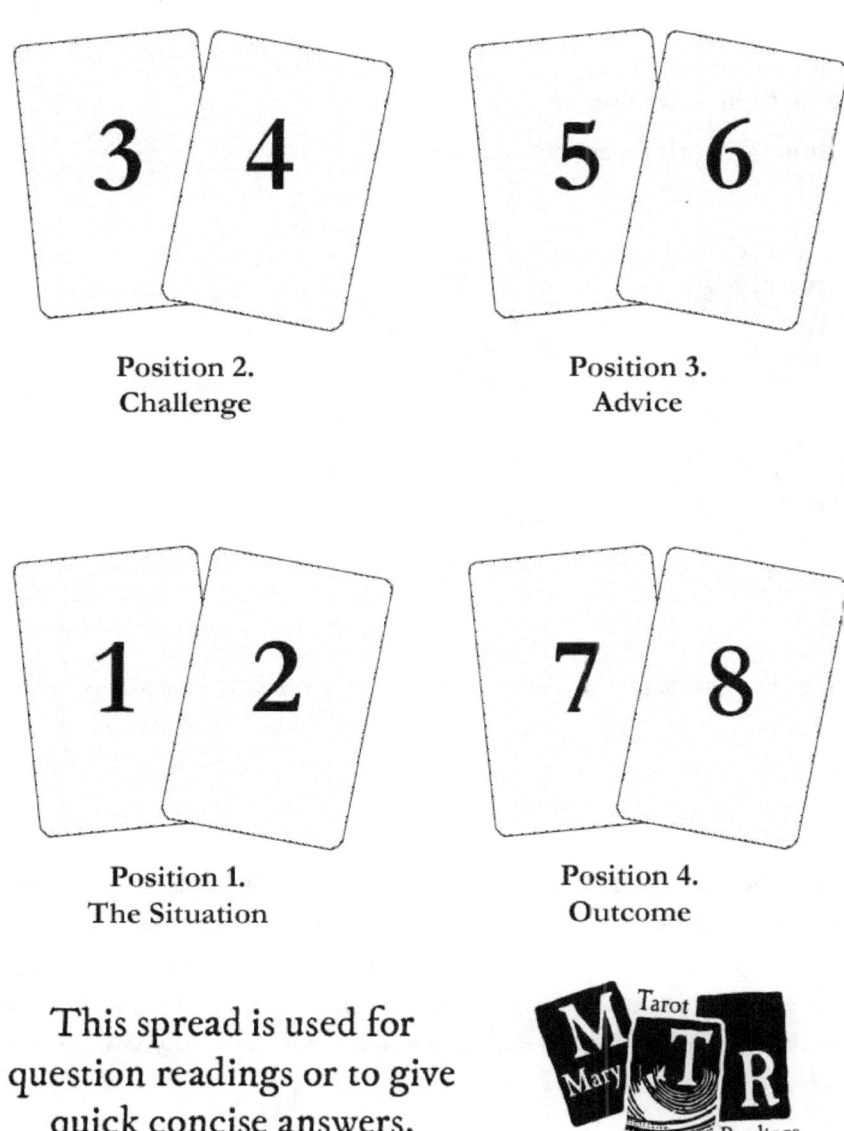

Position 2.
Challenge

Position 3.
Advice

Position 1.
The Situation

Position 4.
Outcome

This spread is used for question readings or to give quick concise answers.

1. The situation

2. The challenge

3. Advice

4. Probable outcome

Example Eight Card Spread

Question: "Where is my relationship headed?"

Position 1: The situation (Moon and Five of Pentacles) *Susan is feeling something is wrong. Her boyfriend is being elusive, and she is feeling something is not right. She is feeling emotionally left out in the cold and she is feeling his withdrawal. Susan is feeling emotional and she is quite 'clingy'. Her intuition is powerful, but she is not listening as the Five of Pentacles suggests.*

Position 2: The challenge (Five of Cups, Lovers) *Holy shit, you simply cannot say your boyfriend is having an affair or fling as the card combo has come up to suggest illicit behavior. What do you say? You would be tactful and say his actions are hurting you. You need to trust your intuition. Why is he withdrawing from you? Are you feeling that due to having been betrayed in the past, this is coming up again for you? Is there a need to let go of past issues and forgive the situation - not because you condone the action of others, but to free yourself from the burden of having to carry these deep and hurtful feelings? Forgiveness creates freedom for you.*

Position 3: Advice (Hanged Man, Judgement) *You are sacrificing yourself in this relationship and things are not moving forward. Is this what you want? Instead of moving forward in your life, you are letting others control your fate. Time to work out what is working for you and what isn't. Time for deep soul searching and coming to a cross road.*

Position 4: Probable outcome (King of Wands. Magician) *The man in your life has got a lot of control and power over you. He can be very charismatic. He could sell ice to Eskimos. He will continue to be a major focus in your life if you keep following this path. There is a huge attraction here, but you are so vulnerable and emotional, and you have to ask yourself if this is healthy for you. Only you can answer that. You have free will to change outcomes at all times, and it's time to focus on yourself and your own happiness. If something doesn't feel right, then it isn't. Time to reflect whether the relationship is all that you are seeking.*

You can use this spread for question readings and you can layer with additional cards.

YES OR NO QUESTIONS

Simply use two cards to get your answer.

Two positive cards - Yes

Two negative cards - No

One of each – A maybe but depending on the strength and value of the cards. I usually take this combo as a No.

Examples of Positive Cards: Sun, Star, Magician, Nine of Cups, Nine of Pentacles

Examples of Negative Cards: Death, Tower, Ten of Swords, Nine of Swords, Ten of Wands

CLASSIC HORSESHOE SPREAD

4
4. Attitude of Client regarding question

3
3. Immediate future

5
5. Other influences

2
2. Present events

6
6. Obstacle

1
1. Past events that may be influencing the question

7
7. Likely outcome

1. Past events that may be influencing the question

2. Present events

3. Immediate future / hopes, fears and expectations

4. Attitude of querent regarding the question /areas of conflict

5. Other influences

6. Obstacle

7. Likely outcome

Example Classic Horseshoe Reading #1

Question: "What do I need to know about my job prospects?"

Card 1: Past events that may be influencing the question (SIX OF WANDS) *In the past the client has been held in high esteem by her peers and she has been very successful in her career.*

Card 2: Present events (ACE OF CUPS) *Presently, there is a new beginning; a new role that is emotionally uplifting.*

Card 3: Immediate future / hopes, fears and expectations (FOOL) *This new role is something completely different to what she has been used to, and she needs to take a leap of faith. She may not have the necessary skills, however she should seize the opportunity and say "yes" and work it out later. The Fool always talks about fresh new starts and stepping into unknown territory.*

Card 4: Attitude of querent regarding the question / areas of conflict (EIGHT OF SWORDS) *Due to the role requiring skills that the querent may not have, she has doubts about her abilities and has a lot of internal negative self-talk. She is starting to self-sabotage as her fear of the unknown and comfort zone come to the fore.*

Card 5: Other influences (KING OF WANDS) *There is a male colleague that will be supportive of her. He is fair minded, easy going and has an expansive view of how things should be done. He might be a fire sign or someone that has attributes of someone friendly, who has great ideas and likes to get along with everyone.*

Card 6: Obstacle (KING OF PENTACLES) *An earth sign man may prove to be difficult for the querent. This male may be involved with finance and is a nitpicker and driven by the bottom line. She should be mindful of her alliances and who to trust.*

Card 7: Likely outcome (SIX OF SWORDS) *The six of swords tells me that she will be able to navigate her way through any issues. Her role could also include travel. Overall, this new role looks promising as long as she can think positively and handle any opposing personalities professionally.*

Example Love Horseshoe Reading #2

(with slightly different positional meanings)

Card 1: Past events that could may be influencing the question

Card 2: Present Events

Card 3: Immediate future / hopes, fears and expectations

Card 4: Attitude of querent regarding the question / areas of conflict

Card 5: Other influences

Card 6: Advice or best course of action

Here is an example of how the Horseshoe works in answer to a specific question about a relationship. The client was a woman in her late 20's who had some gnawing doubts about the future of her relationship. Her question was, **"Where is my relationship going"?**

Card 1: Past events that may be influencing the question (THE DEVIL) *This shows that in the past, the relationship had a passionately physical basis and that it tends to be obsessive - certainly on the part of the client. She was initially infatuated with her boyfriend and failed to see him as he really was.*

Card 2: Present events (JUSTICE) *This card clearly demonstrates her need to make a decision to find some kind of balance in the situation and suggests that she would like to marry her boyfriend, rather than simply live with him. But, she still seems to be living in a dream world where the relationship is concerned, for Justice is quite a cold, detached card. She would prefer to be married and would like her boyfriend to agree.*

Card 3: Immediate future / hopes, fears and expectations (SIX OF SWORDS) *Here is further confirmation of her rather unrealistic attitudes towards the relationship. She hopes that marriage will provide her with an escape route; a passage away from difficulties.*

Card 4: Attitude of querent regarding the question /areas of conflict (QUEEN OF WANDS) *The presence of the Queen of Wands suggests that another woman – or the memory of one- is coming between this couple. Indeed, it turned out that the boyfriend had been married before and the client felt insecure about this. However, it also explained the boyfriend's hesitation and fear of making a second mistake.*

Card 5: Other influences (THE HANGED MAN) *This shows the attitudes of other people to our client's dilemma. Clearly, others believe that she has reached a plateau that there is little possibility of her circumstances changing and that progress is suspended for the time being. Some people may believe that she is sacrificing any possibility of getting married by staying with this man. These views are influencing her and confirming her worst fears.*

Card 6: Advice or best course of action (THE HERMIT) *The Hermit highlights the best course of action open to this woman, which is to calm down, be quiet and listen to her own inner voice. Someone is likely to offer wise advice very soon, and she should pay attention to it if she wishes to resolve matters.*

Card 7: Likely outcome (THREE OF CUPS) *Here is the result and final answer to her question. This card suggests a happy outcome, after a period of withdrawal suggested by the Hermit. There is a celebration, and an engagement is likely.*

ASTROLOGY SPREAD

1. The Client. May describe personality, and what they are going through.
2. Money & Possesions. Combine with 8th & 10th houses for full financial/career overview.
3. Local affairs, communication, short trips, courses, siblings, cousins, neighbours.
4. Home, mother, family life, home life, relatives.
5. Children, entertainment, lovers, speculation in business or gambling, father.
6. Work, service, health, hospitals, bosses, employees.
7. Partnerships, relationships, marriage.
8. Shared finances, deep side of life, birth, death. Sex, relationships. Hidden stuff, inheritance.
9. Travel, foreign places and people, religion, higher education, your vision for the future.
10. Status, career, aims, public standing.
11. Friends, clubs, hobbies, associations, charities.
12. Inner-self which includes - what's on your mind, fears, psychic, the occult.

I use this spread to give me an overview of the person's life and the energy around all spheres of life. I believe it is the best spread for an overview, but you of course can then drill down to a certain area to obtain more detail. It is not the easiest spread for a beginner, as there is a lot to remember, however the value in this reading will cover almost every aspect of the client's life. It draws the reader's attention to the problematical sections of the client's current situation. Please find below, a quick clue summary of the houses in an easy to read format.

The Twelve Houses
(representing the areas and experiences in life)
First House: The Client. The body and appearance, People closely affecting the questioner if court cards fall here. It advises you what is happening around the person's life right now and up to approximately 4-8 weeks in influence.
Second House: Money and possessions, values. Please note: look at the tenth house, as there is a link here, as the tenth house rules career or what you do in life.
Third House: Local affairs, communication, short trips, study (Tafe or courses), siblings and neighbours.
Fourth House: Home, mother, family life, home life, relatives.
Fifth House: Children, entertainment, lovers, speculation in business or gambling (I often see wins in here through luck).
Sixth House: Work/service, health, hospitals, bosses and employees.
Seventh House: Partnerships, relationships, marriage.
Eighth House: Shared finances, deep side of life, birth and death, sex, relationships where sex is important, hidden and closet stuff, wills, estates, matters to do with other people's money.
Ninth House: Travel, foreign places and people, religion /mysticism, higher education, your vision for the future and what you are looking for.
Tenth House: Status, career, aims, father (sometimes the father can also apply in the fifth house - there are two modes of thoughts on this one).
Eleventh House: Friends, clubs, hobbies, associations.
Twelfth House: Inner self which includes what's on your mind, fears, peace. Psychic/mediumship

Example Astrological Spread #1

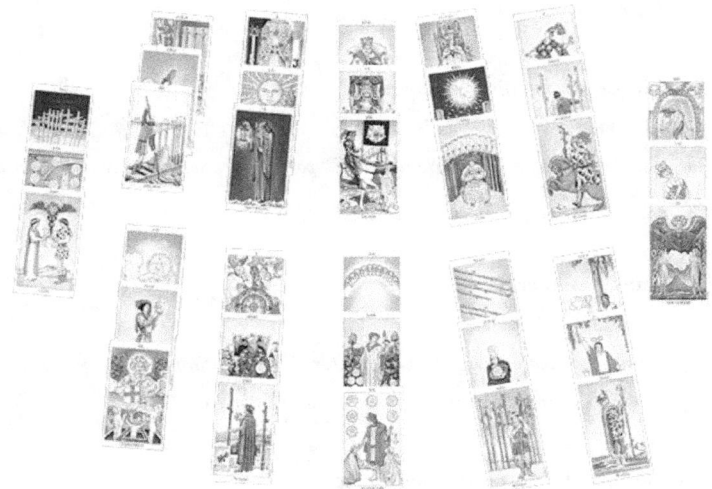

Draw three cards for each house, starting with the First House in sequence.

Tip: Remember to look for major arcana cards first - there are thirteen. Take note where they fall, as this will highlight key points of the reading.

Following major cards, look for negative cards to let you know the challenges the client maybe facing.

Any sequences, card combos?

First House – Current energy/information about the client
Cards: Ten of Swords, Ten of Pentacles, Two of Cups

The Client maybe concluding financial or property matters. Take note that there are two tens, so it's giving strength to the timing as being close to finalization. Also, look at the Second House by linking the Judgement card, which talks about concluding matters and being at a cross road in terms of financial affairs. The Two of Cups tells me that a contract or deal will be concluded. If I had to give it timing, I would say it would be concluded in a short time frame, if not already concluded.

Second House – Finances
Cards: Ace of Pentacles, Page of Pentacles, Judgement

A lump sum of money could be on the cards and there's a need to make decisions about what to do. The Judgement card is saying that the client needs to evaluate what's important and move on. Also, matters to do with financial wellbeing of children are indicated. Look at the Eighth House - it looks like a possible home move/investment and exploring new opportunities (Fool is a new venture and Three of Wands is opportunities - perhaps in collaboration with others. Since it has fallen in the Eighth house of joint finances, the word 'joint' is highlighted).

Third House – Short trips, study, communication, siblings

Cards: Wheel of Fortune, King of Pentacles, Two of Wands

Contacts/advice regarding settlements could be forthcoming. An earth sign male - possibly an accountant - could be offering work or advice adding value in some way.

Fourth House – Home, motherhood, mother, family life

Cards: Ten of Cups, Nine of Pentacles, Six of Pentacles

Around the area of home, the energy is very loving and a feeling of abundance here. There is a feeling also of getting rid of furniture or giving to charity (Six of Pentacles). Life is settled, and things are flowing ahead nicely.

Fifth House – Romance, recreation, children, fatherhood, father

Cards- Eight of Wands, Four of Pentacles, Nine of Wands

Busy social life - lots of activity and invitations. There is also a focus on children and children's activities. With the Nine of Wands, it tells me that there is a lot of effort expended. Why do I pick up a need for routine? At this stage, I'm pondering as this is the romance section, so let's take a look at the Seventh House also in conjunction with the Sixth House below.

Sixth House – Health, work, duty, service to others, side businesses

Cards- Four of Cups, Magician, Page of Wands

The Four of Cups tells me the client may suffer a bit of depression or is feeling a bit flat. The client may get bored easily and needs to keep an active mind. The Magician falling in the health house talks about nervous energy, so reading to relax (Page of Wands) or engaging in a sport will help. The Magician being someone who specialises in the area of health or wellbeing, could be helpful to the person having a reading.

Seventh House – Partnerships, relationships, marriage

Cards: The Lovers, Strength, The World

I would say there is or will be a soul mate connection with a really kind, good looking male who is worldly - sometimes the person in question may have an overseas connection. This tells me that in the area of relationship or love, things are going to be big (three majors here) but perhaps at the point when the client wants to chuck it in (Nine of Wands) in the sense that she has had enough of the dating scene or with love in general.

Eighth House – Sex, death, joint finances, money that incorporates other people, subconscious/hidden

Cards: The Fool, Three of Wands, Knight of Wands

Subconsciously, lots of ideas and planning happening. Looks like a new job - also look at the Tenth House which has the Death card here. An ending and a new beginning. Look at all the cards clustering this top section - The Moon, Death, Hermit, High Priestess and court cards tells me that mediumship is very strong for this person and they could step forward and read for other people. I feel that an older male is stepping through to guide her at this time. He feels like a grandfatherly sort of figure.

Ninth House – Study, higher education, philosophy, travel, long-term view about future

Cards: The Moon, Queen of Wands, Nine of Cups

The client is an Empath and needs to judge things by the way she feels. She will succeed in the psychic field. The Nine of Cups tells me that her wish for the future will be fulfilled. There are also heightened visions and dreams at this time.

Tenth House – Career, ambition, status, public image, father figures

Cards: King of Cups, The Chariot, Death

There is an ending here; perhaps an association with a male. A change of direction is likely and wanting to take control of your career, and where you are headed. I feel things are still unclear - look at the High Priestess and the Moon enveloping this area. Things are yet to unfold. Learning, teaching and spiritual development are highlighted. Mediumship or spirit trying to connect through this reading is strong. This house is related to father figures, so this would show you that a male is trying to connect to this client. As an after note, the client confirmed her grandad had recently passed and was on her mind. Now, we don't need cards to connect to spirit as we can connect directly with them, but they can make their presence known through the tarot. I have seen this over and over.

Eleventh House – Causes, groups, association, friends and friendships

Cards: The High Priestess, The Sun, The Hermit

Friendships are forged again within the spiritual industry. Also, joining likeminded groups for spiritual development are highlighted. Enrichment around friendships. Learning and study is important. Going to a meditation circle, and doing yoga are amplified.

Twelfth House – What's on your mind (real concern), psychic ability, occult, what's hidden

Cards: Four of Swords, Two of Pentacles, Six of Pentacles

The Four of Swords tells me that client may need to step back and relax as there is a lot of juggling happening. Also, this talks about taking a trip away as a break. The person can look forward to more peaceful times ahead if she can take time to relax and prioritize, and not take too much on.

Mediumship Cards: The High Priestess, Ace of Swords, Death, The Magician, The Moon

RELATIONSHIP SPREAD

1. Client
His/Her feelings
towards the other person

2. Partner/Other Person
His/Her feelings
towards the other person

**3. Challenges to the
relationship**

**3. Challenges to the
relationship**

**5. What connects them.
Common values.**

**6. Where the relationship
is headed.**

RELATIONSHIP READINGS

Most people want to know either where their relationship is heading, or when they are going to meet someone. It is a highly emotional area and you need to tread lightly with how you deliver these messages. Remember to deliver insights or messages in a way that is empowering for the client to make up their own mind. Sometimes you see endings and it is very clear; other times it can be messages of encouragement to see the appropriate professional and that may or may not be you. If it is a difficult reading, still provide solutions as there is always something to be grateful for, or a lesson to overcome. Sometimes, a kind ear is more appropriate than being harsh if someone is not mentally ready to accept what you are saying. This is not to embellish the reading, but it is better to be kind than to be right at the expense of someone's mental health. Choose your words wisely.

1. Client feelings
2. Partner feelings
3. Challenges/issues (client's perspective)
4. Challenges/issues (partner's perspective)
5. Common interests/what brings them together
6. Likely Outcome

You can layer cards, therefore drawing twelve or eighteen cards, but to begin with, I would read with six cards only.

Top Cards for Relationships

Ten of Cups, Two of Cups, Four of Wands (engagement or wedding)

Hierophant (marriage or commitment)

The Lovers, Ace of Cups (new love or resurgence of love)

Ten of Pentacles (building a family or long-term plans)

The Sun (general happiness)

The Star (fidelity)

Trouble in Paradise Cards (combinations)

Five of Cups plus The Lovers (affair)

Five of Swords (tit for tat arguing)

The Moon plus Seven of Swords (deceit and lies)

Timing in Tarot

You can use the various suits to try to pin down timing. Also look at the card images and colours. Is it cold? Are the colours warm and summery? Below is the most common method for timing.

Wands: Days or Summer
Swords: Weeks or Spring
Cups: Months or Autumn
Pentacles: Years or Winter

In addition, here are some additional tips:

A run of numbers will also give you an indication of the month, e.g. a run of 8's could mean August (eighth month).

Nine of Wands: just around the corner could be one week as it is a $9 + 1 = 10$ (full cycle) so this gives you one week. The meaning of this card is also 'don't throw in the towel - there is a breakthrough coming'.

Use Astrological associations for timing, e.g. Queen of Pentacles, Nine of Cups. This Queen is an earth sign, but the month being next to the Nine of Cups would be the ninth month, which indicates Virgo or September.

When **The Emperor** sits on his throne, does he remind you of Father Christmas? Look at the numerical numbers of the cards (remember the Pages are numbered 11, Knights 12, Queens 13, Kings 14)

It's not just about the card meanings - it's about using your intuition to take readings to a new level.

Reading the tarot is so much more than card meanings, although you do need to start somewhere. Begin by trusting your intuition, look at the colour in cards, take notice of numerical sequences, psychic flashes, or energy shifts that could mean spirit communication through mediumship. Look for card combos and develop your own tarot words through your own card combinations. When you feel confident, you can layer cards to give readings more depth and often this shows patterns and events that we must go through in our journey.

The tarot is simply one of many tools to enhance and develop your intuition. You may use this as your main tool, or to compliment another existing modality. When reading the tarot, listen to your intuition in defining the meanings of the cards to give them more depth. If you look at a card and receive an impression, do not discount it. Have the faith and courage to say what you see.

Look at the colours of the cards. What impressions do you receive? Do they correlate with the colours of the chakras or give you impression of a sunny destination or a cold climate? The possibilities are endless. Even if it doesn't make sense to you, it might make sense or be meaningful to the person you are reading for. Once you miss the moment to deliver the message, you have missed it.

Look at the numbers. Are they repetitive? You can explore the meanings through numerology or even Doreen Virtue's Angel Numbers. Repetitive numbers could indicate timing in a reading if a client asks for timing. It could also indicate which stage of a situation a person is in, e.g. lots of tens could mean the client is at the end of a cycle.

The tarot may stimulate psychic flashes or even mediumship. Again, do not discount it and be brave enough to mention what you hear, feel, see, taste (we refer to these senses as 'clairs'). There are some card combinations that show someone in spirit is trying to connect. If you hear a name, it could be the actual spirit or a connection to that spirit. This could propel you into a mediumship reading, where you stop reading the cards and merge your energy with spirit to convey messages or evidence of the afterlife.

You will also start to get your own card combos that help you build deeper and more meaningful stories. An idea is to take a photo of your spreads, so when you receive feedback you can relook at your spread to see how the card combos fit, or how you could have interpreted it differently. Just know that whatever you said was right at the time, so please don't beat yourself up.

Layering cards is an alternate method instead of using reversals. As the cards heighten or diminish the card, they are either against, or change its meaning, e.g. Strength with the Devil against it would tell me a person's energy is diminished or their resilience is under pressure. If on the other hand, the Sun was against the Strength card, it magnifies the qualities of this card.

Helpful Tips

1. Scan the spread. How many major cards are there?

2. Are there challenge cards, i.e. Swords or negative cards?

3. For relationship readings, do you have many positive Cup cards or 'love cards'?

4. For career readings, do you have many Wands or Pentacle cards to denote movement/advancement or increased wealth?

5. Court cards - how many? Are they well aspected? Will they help or hinder your client or yourself?

6. Any numerical sequences, colors etc.?

7. Recognise any card combos?

8. If using the astrological spread, do any cards fall in their natural house or association? e.g. Devil in the Eighth House (sex addiction). If the World card fell in Ninth House of travel, it is definitely relating to an overseas trip. A card falling in its natural house will give you a precise and accurate interpretation.

Also…

If cards don't talk to you, don't worry about it - move on. Use that card to meditate on for a few days.

Use a journal and write down reflections following your daily card.

Take mental notes of feedback and relate it back to your reading. You may want to take photos for reference while you are learning. You will find the tarot will start to talk, so you clearly understand the messages.

Use summary lists if you need to while you are learning, but it's only necessary to learn one or two key words. Don't make it hard for yourself. It's not an exact science.

Until Next Time…

I hope the 'The Little Book of Tarot' has inspired you to have more confidence in reading tarot intuitively. Whilst there are basic meanings to the 78 cards, as you learn and grow as a reader your tarot vocabulary will grow. This book has covered traditional meanings, the importance of looking at card combos or linking cards for greater accuracy, case studies, and basic spreads, as well as the more advanced Astrology Spread.

If I could save you some heartbreak with tarot, is not to expect one hundred percent accuracy - it is not possible. We are human; we may interpret something that is not quite right, or spirit may not want to show an event because it is not for the client's highest good or growth. Remember that we have free will to change the course of our lives. The tarot will tune into the energy at play at the time and based on this energy, will give you a projected outcome.

Tarot has been a long-life passion of mine and I know it will become yours too. We are forever learning something new. Your client is also your teacher. You will become aware of themes or attracting the same type of clients. You may want to check in with your own energy. There will be synchronicity with readings. If you are reading for yourself, you will get the same message until the event occurs or you take the advice. That's how tarot rolls. When you get discouraged with readings or people you are reading for might say "no" just remember that not everyone is open to being told something they are not prepared to hear. Just let it go - it's not your job to convince anyone. You are simply a messenger. You job is just to have faith in the process and in your own abilities. Take a reality check on all the times you got it right.

Some people say, "You are only as good as your last reading". I prefer my saying of, "Treat every reading like it was your first".

Wishing you the best on your Tarot journey,

Mary

Keywords

The best way to get familiar with your 78 cards is to remember a keyword or two for each card (keep it simple – two at most). I found when I was learning, I would write down each of the cards, then try to write the meaning beside it. I have found that this is the best way to remember. Before it can stimulate your intuition, you need to know the basic meanings.

You can use these keyword tables to refer to while you're learning the tarot, and you'll find an exercise later in the book where you can create your own keywords.

MAJOR ARCANA

	Upright	Reversed
	New beginning /path, freedom	Foolish, risk taking
	Skill, power, manifesting	Poor planning, manipulative
	Intuition, spiritual guidance	Undiscerning, unaware, deceit
	Fertility, abundance	Barren, lack of abundance
	Authority, structures	Domineering, controlling
	Tradition, values, religion	Rebellious, not conforming
	Love, soulmates, choices, values	Disharmony, poor choices
	Victory, success, determination	Lack of direction and control
	Patience, forgiveness,	No patience, feeling weak
	Advice, inner guidance	Loneliness, not listening to advice
	Fate, turn of events, lady luck	Feeling unlucky, unfortunate events

	Justice, law, truth, fairness	Injustice, unfairness
	Delays, needing to surrender	Martyrdom
	Endings, new beginnings	Resistance to change
	Balance, healing, compromise	Imbalance, lack of compromise
	Happiness, children, love	Unhappy, failure
	Materialism, addictions, sex	Detachment from addiction or control
	Sudden change, upheaval	Disruption, resisting changes
	Hope, faith, renewal	Losing hope, desperation
	Dreams, subconscious	Confusion, deceit
	Life review, judgement	Inability to see things how they are
	Completion, success, travel	Inability to finish things or lack of closure

MINOR ARCANA

	PENTACLES	WANDS	CUPS	SWORDS
Ace	Monetary gains, new job, loans, lump sum R: Material problems	New job, new creative outlets R: Stifled ambition	New love, resurgence of love, inspiration R: Emotional upheaval	Clarity, epiphany, truth R: Tension
2	Juggling money, two steams of income R: Financial disarray	Plans, progress, help is coming, Partnerships R: Plans not working	Relationship, partnership R: Disharmony	stalemate, minor delays R: Indecision
3	Promotion, collaboration, trades, team work R: Lack of teamwork	New opportunities, looking forward R: Lack of foresight	Celebrations, good news, friends, events R: Over indulging	Tears, heartbreak, arguments R: Releasing Pain
4	Financial security, savings, frugality R: Materialism	Home, celebrations, family life, real estate R: Family problems	Apathy, lack of interest, reflection R: Boredom	Rest and recuperation, taking a break R: Enforced rest
5	Financial loss, unemployment or feeling emotionally void R: Financial recovery	Arguments, competition, banter, conflict R: Lack of conviction	Upset, regret, mourning the past, hurt, wounded R: Moving on	Conflict, defeat, winning, violence R: Battle of Wills
6	Charity, energy exchanges, non for profit, paying it forward R: Uncharitable	Accolades, recognition and reward, advancement, Good reputation, referrals R: Tarnished Reputation, self-worth	The past, happy memories, reunions. The past could be helpful R: Stuck in the past	Calm after storm, peace, travel, looking forward R: Inability to move on
7	Needing to persevere. Long term investment. R: Inability to see the big picture or long term view	Overwhelm, defending your position, feeling challenged R: Giving up	Too many options, confusion, all that glistens are not gold. R: Delusional	Deceit, liar, gossip, temporary, avoidance R: Mental challenges

8	Creating wealth through hard work, courses, accreditation R: Lack of focus and application	Swift action, activity, travel, expansion, Yes R: Slow, delays	Turning your back and walking away. Wanting change. R: hopelessness	Mental anguish, feeling restricted and focusing on the negative. R: Open to new perspectives
9	Material comfort and gain. Receiving the rewards of past investment. Satisfaction R: Feeling dissatisfied	Wanting to throw in the towel. Nearing the completion of cycles. Time to tie up loose ends. R: Not worth the effort	Wishes coming true. Happiness. Goals achieved. Feeling smug R: Not happy	Stress, worry, broken sleep. Not being able to see solutions R; Release from fear
10	Family Business, Family, Inheritance, Investments R: Issues with family or relating to family money or inheritances	Carrying a burden, responsibility, a block R: Welcoming responsibility, overcoming blocks or burdens lessening	Happiness, joy, relationship. Love R: Unhappy, unloved or issues around relationships	Anguish, stress, end of cycle it can only get better R: Resisting an ending or not wanting to seek solutions for your problem, staying in victimhood
Page	News, minor financial improvement, a child/younger person One step at a time R: Little things bother you, introversion	News, messenger, books, creativity, a child/younger person R: Minor setbacks to plans	News, birth of a child, psychic flashes, child/young person R: Emotional immaturity	News with a gossipy overtone. Child/younger person. Study, intellect, communication, R: Spiteful
Knight	Steady progress, young male, steady job, safe option R: laziness, unreliable	Job offer, house move, travel, new energy, drive, young impulsive male, action R: Haste	New love coming into your life, an offer, knight in shining armour, young sensitive male R: Moodiness	Hasty decisions, needing to think on your feet, young man who acts before the thinks R: Lack of regard for consequences
Queen	Down to earth woman. Being practical. Financial growth through analyzing	A determined woman who is fierce but loyal. Leadership qualities	Often appears as a mother figure or a woman related by marriage. Sensitive, intuitive and emotional.	Intellectual, independent woman. This queen rules communication and anything to do with intellectual pursuits

	R: Being Critical	R: Domineering and aggressive	R: Over emotional woman	R: Bitch
King	Financial success. Mature male who is financially secure. Power is expressed through success in finances. R: Miserly and controlling	Leadership, entrepreneur, fairness, easy going, strategist, visionary. A man's man Power through leadership R: Nothing will get in his way- ruthless, player	Can sometimes represent father figures or men related. Sensitive men or those more in touch with their feelings. R: Moody	Intellectual male with degree. This King rules communication and having clarity. Power of the mind R: Mentally abusive

Your Keywords

MAJOR ARCANA

The Fool:	
The Magician:	
The High Priestess:	
The Empress:	
The Emperor:	
The Hierophant:	
The Lovers:	
The Chariot:	
Strength:	
The Hermit:	
The Wheel of Fortune:	
Justice:	
The Hanged Man:	
Death:	
Temperance:	
The Devil:	
The Tower:	
The Star:	
The Moon:	
The Sun:	
Judgment:	
The World:	

WANDS	
Ace of Wands:	
Two of Wands:	
Three of Wands:	
Four of Wands:	
Five of Wands:	
Six of Wands:	
Seven of Wands:	
Eight of Wands:	
Nine of Wands:	
Ten of Wands:	
Page of Wands:	
Knight of Wands:	
Queen of Wands:	
King of Wands:	
CUPS	
Ace of Cups:	
Two of Cups:	
Three of Cups:	
Four of Cups:	
Five of Cups:	
Six of Cups:	
Seven of Cups:	
Eight of Cups:	
Nine of Cups:	
Ten of Cups:	
Page of Cups:	
Knight of Cups:	
Queen of Cups:	
King of Cups:	

SWORDS	
Ace of Swords:	
Two of Swords:	
Three of Swords:	
Four of Swords:	
Five of Swords:	
Six of Swords:	
Seven of Swords:	
Eight of Swords:	
Nine of Swords:	
Ten of Swords:	
Page of Swords:	
Knight of Swords:	
Queen of Swords:	
King of Swords:	
PENTACLES	
Ace of Pentacles:	
Two of Pentacles:	
Three of Pentacles:	
Four of Pentacles:	
Five of Pentacles:	
Six of Pentacles:	
Seven of Pentacles:	
Eight of Pentacles:	
Nine of Pentacles:	
Ten of Pentacles:	
Page of Pentacles:	
Knight of Pentacles:	
Queen of Pentacles:	
King of Pentacles:	

A few more tidbits…

It's okay if some cards don't connect with you. Put them aside in a pile and spend some time on these cards over the following weeks. Then, come back and write down a few key meanings.

Use keywords of the cards to answer your questions and remember to let the cards talk to you. Even if you get one word, sometimes that is enough to satisfy which direction someone should be taking.

It is important as you connect to the card to listen to your intuition. Your first intuitive response is often the correct one.

Once you connect certain words to the tarot cards, they will start to appear for you over and over, so you can easily put stories together and give sound guidance and even predictions.